CHRISTIAN HEALING

THE PEOPLE'S IDEA OF GOD

PULPIT AND PRESS

CHRISTIAN SCIENCE VERSUS PANTHEISM

MESSAGE TO THE MOTHER CHURCH, 1900

MESSAGE TO THE MOTHER CHURCH, 1901

MESSAGE TO THE MOTHER CHURCH, 1902

CHRISTIAN HEALING

A SERMON DELIVERED AT BOSTON

CHRISTIAN HEALING

BY

MARY BAKER EDDY

AUTHOR OF SCIENCE AND HEALTH WITH KEY TO THE
SCRIPTURES

A SERMON DELIVERED AT BOSTON

Registered
U. S. Patent Office

Published by The
Trustees under the Will of Mary Baker G. Eddy
BOSTON, U. S. A.

Authorized Literature of
THE FIRST CHURCH OF CHRIST, SCIENTIST
in Boston, Massachusetts

PRINTED IN THE UNITED STATES OF AMERICA

SERMON

SUBJECT

CHRISTIAN HEALING

TEXT: *And these signs shall follow them that believe; In my name shall they cast out devils; they shall speak with new tongues; they shall take up serpents; and if they drink any deadly thing, it shall not hurt them; they shall lay hands on the sick, and they shall recover.* — MARK XVI. 17, 18.

HISTORY repeats itself; to-morrow grows out of to-day. But Heaven's favors are formidable: they are calls to higher duties, not discharge from care; and whoso builds on less than an immortal basis, hath built on sand.

We have asked, in our selfishness, to wait until the age advanced to a more practical and spiritual religion before arguing with the world the great subject of Christian healing; but our answer was, "Then there were no cross to take up, and less need of publishing the good news." A classic writes, —

> "At thirty, man suspects himself a fool;
> Knows it at forty, and reforms his plan;
> At fifty, chides his infamous delay,
> Pushes his prudent purpose to resolve."

The difference between religions is, that one religion has a more spiritual basis and tendency than the other; and the religion nearest right is that one. The genius of Christianity is works more than words; a calm and steadfast communion with God; a tumult on earth, — religious factions and prejudices arrayed against it, the synagogues as of old closed upon it, while it reasons with the storm, hurls the thunderbolt of truth, and stills the tempest of error; scourged and condemned at every advancing footstep, afterwards pardoned and adopted, but never seen amid the smoke of battle. Said the intrepid reformer, Martin Luther: "I am weary of the world, and the world is weary of me; the parting will be easy." Said the more gentle Melanchthon: "Old Adam is too strong for young Melanchthon."

And still another Christian hero, ere he passed from his execution to a crown, added his testimony: "I have fought a good fight, . . . I have kept the faith." But Jesus, the model of infinite patience, said: "Come unto me, all ye that labor and are heavy laden, and I will give you rest." And he said this when bending beneath the malice of the world. But why should the world hate Jesus, the loved of the Father, the loved of Love? It was that his spirituality rebuked their carnality, and gave this proof of Christianity that religions had not given. Again, they knew it was not in the power of eloquence or a dead rite to cast out error and heal the sick. Past, present, future magnifies his name who built, on Truth, eternity's foundation stone, and sprinkled the altar of Love with perpetual incense.

Such Christianity requires neither hygiene nor drugs
wherewith to heal both mind and body; or, lacking these,
to show its helplessness. The primitive privilege of Christianity was to make men better, to cast out error, and heal
the sick. It was a proof, more than a profession thereof;
a demonstration, more than a doctrine. It was the foundation of right thinking and right acting, and must be
reestablished on its former basis. The stone which the
builders rejected must again become the head of the
corner. In proportion as the personal and material element stole into religion, it lost Christianity and the power
to heal; and the qualities of God as a person, instead of
the divine Principle that begets the quality, engrossed the
attention of the ages. In the original text the term *God*
was derived from the word *good*. Christ is the idea
of Truth; Jesus is the name of a man born in a remote
province of Judea, — Josephus alludes to several individuals by the name of Jesus. Therefore Christ Jesus was
an honorary title; it signified a "good man," which epi-
thet the great goodness and wonderful works of our
Master more than merited. Because God is the Principle of
Christian healing, we must understand in part this divine
Principle, or we cannot demonstrate it in part.

The Scriptures declare that "God is Love, Truth, and
Life," — a trinity in unity; not three persons in one, but
three statements of one Principle. We cannot tell what is
the person of Truth, the body of the infinite, but we know
that the Principle is not the person, that the finite cannot

1 contain the infinite, that unlimited Mind cannot start from
a limited body. The infinite can neither go forth from,
3 return to, nor remain for a moment within limits. We
must give freer breath to thought before calculating the
results of an infinite Principle, — the effects of infinite
6 Love, the compass of infinite Life, the power of infinite
Truth. Clothing Deity with personality, we limit the action of God to the finite senses. We pray for God to re-
9 member us, even as we ask a person with softening of the
brain not to forget his daily cares. We ask infinite wisdom
to possess our finite sense, and forgive what He knows
12 deserves to be punished, and to bless what is unfit to be
blessed. We expect infinite Love to drop divinity long
enough to hate. We expect infinite Truth to mix with
15 error, and become finite for a season; and, after infinite
Spirit is forced in and out of matter for an indefinite period,
to show itself infinite again. We expect infinite Life to
18 become finite, and have an end; but, after a temporary
lapse, to begin anew as infinite Life, without beginning and
without end.

21   Friends, can we ever arrive at a proper conception of the
divine character, and gain a right idea of the Principle of
all that is right, with such self-evident contradictions?
24 God must be our model, or we have none; and if this
model is one thing at one time, and the opposite of it at
another, can we rely on our model? Or, having faith in it,
27 how can we demonstrate a changing Principle? We cannot: we shall be consistent with our inconsistent statement

of Deity, and so bring out our own erring finite sense of God, and of good and evil blending. While admitting that God is omnipotent, we shall be limiting His power at every point, — shall be saying He is beaten by certain kinds of food, by changes of temperature, the neglect of a bath, and so on. Phrenology will be saying the developments of the brain bias a man's character. Physiology will be saying, if a man has taken cold by doing good to his neighbor, God will punish him now for the cold, but he must wait for the reward of his good deed hereafter. One of our leading clergymen startles us by saying that "between Christianity and spiritualism, the question chiefly is concerning the trustworthiness of the communications, and not the doubt of their reality." Does any one think the departed are not departed, but are with us, although we have no evidence of the fact except sleight-of-hand and hallucination?

Such hypotheses ignore Biblical authority, obscure the one grand truth which is constantly covered, in one way or another, from our sight. This truth is, that we are to work out our own salvation, and to meet the responsibility of our own thoughts and acts; relying not on the person of God or the person of man to do our work for us, but on the apostle's rule, "I will show thee my faith by my works." This spiritualism would lead our lives to higher issues; it would purify, elevate, and consecrate man; it would teach him that "whatsoever a man soweth, that shall he also reap." The more spiritual we become

1 here, the more are we separated from the world; and
should this rule fail hereafter, and we grow more material,
3 and so come back to the world? When I was told the other
day, "People say you are a medium," pardon me if I
smiled. The pioneer of something new under the sun is
6 never hit: he cannot be; the opinions of people fly too
high or too low. From my earliest investigations of the
mental phenomenon named mediumship, I knew it was
9 misinterpreted, and I said it. The spiritualists abused me
for it then, and have ever since; but they take pleasure in
calling me a medium. I saw the impossibility, in Science,
12 of intercommunion between the so-called dead and the
living. When I learned how mind produces disease on the
body, I learned how it produces the manifestations ig-
15 norantly imputed to spirits. I saw how the mind's ideals
were evolved and made tangible; and it matters not
whether that ideal is a flower or a cancer, if the belief is
18 strong enough to manifest it. Man thinks he is a medium
of disease; that when he is sick, disease controls his body
to whatever manifestation we see. But the fact remains,
21 in metaphysics, that the mind of the individual only can
produce a result upon his body. The belief that produces
this result may be wholly unknown to the individual, be-
24 cause it is lying back in the unconscious thought, a latent
cause producing the effect we see.

"And these signs shall follow them that believe; In
27 my name shall they cast out devils." The word *devil*
comes from the Greek *diabolos;* in Hebrew it is *belial,* and

signifies "that which is good for nothing, lust," etc. The
signs referred to are the manifestations of the power of
Truth to cast out error; and, correcting error in thought,
it produces the harmonious effect on the body. "Them
that believe" signifies those who understand God's supremacy, — the power of Mind over matter. "The new
tongue" is the spiritual meaning as opposed to the material.
It is the language of Soul instead of the senses; it translates
matter into its original language, which is Mind, and gives
the spiritual instead of the material signification. It begins
with motive, instead of act, where Jesus formed his estimate; and there correcting the motive, it corrects the act
that results from the motive. The Science of Christianity
makes pure the fountain, in order to purify the stream. It
begins in mind to heal the body, the same as it begins in
motive to correct the act, and through which to judge of it.
The Master of metaphysics, reading the mind of the poor
woman who dropped her mite into the treasury, said,
"She hath cast in more than they all." Again, he charged
home a crime to mind, regardless of any outward act, and
sentenced it as our judges would not have done to-day.
Jesus knew that adultery is a crime, and *mind* is the crim-
inal. I wish the age was up to his understanding of these
two facts, so important to progress and Christianity.

"They shall take up serpents; and if they drink any
deadly thing, it shall not hurt them." This is an unquali-
fied statement of the duty and ability of Christians to heal
the sick; and it contains no argument for a creed or doc-

1 trine, it implies no necessity beyond the understanding of
God, and obedience to His government, that heals both
3 mind and body; God, — not a person to whom we should
pray to heal the sick, but the Life, Love, and Truth that
destroy error and death. Understanding the truth regard-
6 ing mind and body, knowing that Mind can master sickness as well as sin, and carrying out this government over
both and bringing out the results of this higher Chris-
9 tianity, we shall perceive the meaning of the context,
— "They shall lay hands on the sick, and they shall
recover."

12   The world is slow to perceive individual advancement;
but when it reaches the thought that has produced this,
then it is willing to be made whole, and no longer quarrels
15 with the individual. Plato did better; he said, "What
thou seest, that thou beest."

The mistaken views entertained of Deity becloud the
18 light of revelation, and suffocate reason by materialism.
When we understand that God is what the Scriptures have
declared, — namely, Life, Truth, and Love, — we shall
21 learn to reach heaven through Principle instead of a pardon; and this will make us honest and laborious, knowing
that we shall receive only what we have earned. Jesus
24 illustrated this by the parable of the husbandman. If we
work to become Christians as honestly and as directly
upon a divine Principle, and adhere to the rule of this
27 Principle as directly as we do to the rule of mathematics,
we shall be Christian Scientists, and do more than we are

now doing, and progress faster than we are now pro- 1
gressing. We should have no anxiety about what is or
what is not the person of God, if we understood the 3
Principle better and employed our thoughts more in demonstrating it. We are constantly thinking and talking
on the wrong side of the question. The less said or thought 6
of sin, sickness, or death, the better for mankind, morally
and physically. The greatest sinner and the most hopeless invalid think most of sickness and of sin; but, having 9
learned that this method has not saved them from either,
why do they go on thus, and their moral advisers talk for
them on the very subjects they would gladly discontinue to 12
bring out in their lives? Contending for the reality of
what should disappear is like furnishing fuel for the flames.
Is it a duty for any one to believe that "the curse causeless 15
cannot come"? Then it is a higher duty to know that
God never cursed man, His own image and likeness. God
never made a wicked man; and man made by God had not 18
a faculty or power underived from his Maker wherewith to
make himself wicked.

The only correct answer to the question, "Who is 21
the author of evil?" is the scientific statement that
evil is unreal; that God made all that was made, but
He never made sin or sickness, either an error of mind 24
or of body. Life in matter is a dream: sin, sickness,
and death are this dream. Life is Spirit; and when we
waken from the dream of life in matter, we shall learn this 27
grand truth of being. St. John saw the vision of life in

1 matter; and he saw it pass away, — an illusion. The
dragon that was wroth with the woman, and stood ready
3 "to devour the child as soon as it was born," was the vision
of envy, sensuality, and malice, ready to devour the idea
of Truth. But the beast bowed before the Lamb: it was
6 supposed to have fought the manhood of God, that Jesus
represented; but it fell before the womanhood of God,
that presented the highest ideal of Love. Let us re-
9 member that God — good — is omnipotent; therefore evil
is impotent. There is but one side to good, — it has no
evil side; there is but one side to reality, and that is the
12 good side.

God is All, and in all: that finishes the question of
a good and a bad side to existence. Truth is the real;
15 error is the unreal. You will gather the importance of
this saying, when sorrow seems to come, if you will look
on the bright side; for sorrow endureth but for the night,
18 and joy cometh with the light. Then will your sorrow be
a dream, and your waking the reality, even the triumph
of Soul over sense. If you wish to be happy, argue with
21 yourself on the side of happiness; take the side you wish
to carry, and be careful not to talk on both sides, or to
argue stronger for sorrow than for joy. You are the at-
24 torney for the case, and will win or lose according to your
plea.

As the mountain hart panteth for the water brooks, so
27 panteth my heart for the true fount and Soul's baptism.
Earth's fading dreams are empty streams, her fountains

play in borrowed sunbeams, her plumes are plucked from
the wings of vanity. Did we survey the cost of sublunary
joy, we then should gladly waken to see it was unreal. A
dream calleth itself a dreamer, but when the dream has
passed, man is seen wholly apart from the dream.

We are in the midst of a revolution; physics are yield-
ing slowly to metaphysics; mortal mind rebels at its own
boundaries; weary of matter, it would catch the meaning
of Spirit. The only immortal superstructure is built on
Truth; her modest tower rises slowly, but it stands and is
the miracle of the hour, though it may seem to the age like
the great pyramid of Egypt, — a miracle in stone. The
fires of ancient proscription burn upon the altars of to-day;
he who has suffered from intolerance is the first to be in-
tolerant. Homœopathy may not recover from the heel of
allopathy before lifting its foot against its neighbor, metaphysics, although homœopathy has laid the foundation
stone of mental healing; it has established this axiom,
"The less medicine the better," and metaphysics adds,
"until you arrive at no medicine." When you have
reached this high goal you have learned that proportionately as matter went out and Mind came in as the remedy,
was its potency. Metaphysics places all cause and cure
as mind; differing in this from homœopathy, where cause
and cure are supposed to be both mind and matter. Metaphysics requires mind imbued with Truth to heal the sick;
hence the Christianity of metaphysical healing, and this
excellence above other systems. The higher attenuations

of homœopathy contain no medicinal properties, and thus it is found out that Mind instead of matter heals the sick.

While the matter-physician feels the pulse, examines the tongue, etc., to learn what matter is doing independent of mind, when it is self-evident it can do nothing, the metaphysician goes to the fount to govern the streams; he diagnoses disease as mind, the basis of all action, and cures it thus when matter cannot cure it, showing he was right. Thus it was we discovered that all physical effects originate in mind before they can become manifest as matter; we learned from the Scripture and Christ's healing that God, directly or indirectly, through His providence or His laws, never made a man sick. When studying the two hundred and sixty remedies of the Jahr, the characteristic peculiarities and the general and moral symptoms requiring the remedy, we saw at once the concentrated power of thought brought to bear on the pharmacy of homœopathy, which made the infinitesimal dose effectual. To prepare the medicine requires time and thought; you cannot shake the poor drug without the involuntary thought, "I am making you more powerful," and the sequel proves it; the higher attenuations prove that the power was the thought, for when the drug disappears by your process the power remains, and homœopathists admit the higher attenuations are the most powerful. The only objection to giving the unmedicated sugar is, it would be dishonest and divide one's faith apparently between

matter and mind, and so weaken both points of action; 1
taking hold of both horns of the dilemma, we should work
at opposites and accomplish less on either side. 3

The pharmacy of homœopathy is reducing the one hun-
dredth part of a grain of medicine two thousand times,
shaking the preparation thirty times at every attenuation. 6
There is a moral to this medicine; the higher natures are
reached soonest by the higher attenuations, until the fact is
found out they have taken no medicine, and then the so- 9
called drug loses its power. We have attenuated a grain of
aconite until it was no longer aconite, then dropped into
a tumblerful of water a single drop of this harmless solu- 12
tion, and administering one teaspoonful of this water at
intervals of half an hour have cured the incipient stage of
fever. The highest attenuation we ever attained was to 15
leave the drug out of the question, using only the sugar of
milk; and with this original dose we cured an inveterate
case of dropsy. After these experiments you cannot be 18
surprised that we resigned the imaginary medicine altogether, and honestly employed Mind as the only curative
Principle. 21

What are the foundations of metaphysical healing?
Mind, divine Science, the truth of being that casts out
error and thus heals the sick. You can readily perceive 24
this mental system of healing is the antipode of mesmerism, Beelzebub. Mesmerism makes one disease while it is
supposed to cure another, and that one is worse than the 27
first; mesmerism is one lie getting the better of another,

1 and the bigger lie occupying the field for a period; it is the
fight of beasts, in which the bigger animal beats the lesser;
3 in fine, much ado about nothing. Medicine will not arrive
at the science of treating disease until disease is treated
mentally and man is healed morally and physically. What
6 has physiology, hygiene, or physics done for Christianity
but to obscure the divine Principle of healing and en-
courage faith in an opposite direction?

9   Great caution should be exercised in the choice of
physicians. If you employ a medical practitioner, be sure
he is a learned man and skilful; never trust yourself in the
12 hands of a quack. In proportion as a physician is enlightened and liberal is he equipped with Truth, and his efforts
are salutary; ignorance and charlatanism are miserable
15 medical aids. Metaphysical healing includes infinitely
more than merely to know that mind governs the body and
the method of a mental practice. The preparation for a
18 metaphysical practitioner is the most arduous task I ever
performed. You must first mentally educate and develop
the spiritual sense or perceptive faculty by which one learns
21 the metaphysical treatment of disease; you must teach
them how to learn, together with what they learn. I
waited many years for a student to reach the ability to
24 teach; it included more than they understood.

      Metaphysical or divine Science reveals the Principle and
method of perfection, — how to attain a mind in harmony
27 with God, in sympathy with all that is right and opposed
to all that is wrong, and a body governed by this mind.

Christian Science repudiates the evidences of the senses
and rests upon the supremacy of God. Christian healing,
established upon this Principle, vindicates the omnipotence of the Supreme Being by employing no other remedy
than Truth, Life, and Love, understood, to heal all ills
that flesh is heir to. It places no faith in hygiene or drugs;
it reposes all faith in mind, in spiritual power divinely
directed. By rightly understanding the power of mind
over matter, it enables mind to govern matter, as it rises
to that supreme sense that shall "take up serpents" un-
harmed, and "if they drink any deadly thing, it shall not
hurt them." Christian Science explains to any one's perfect satisfaction the so-called miracles recorded in the
Bible. Ah! why should man deny all might to the divine
Mind, and claim another mind perpetually at war with this
Mind, when at the same time he calls God almighty and
admits in statement what he denies in proof? You pray
for God to heal you, but should you expect this when you
are acting oppositely to your prayer, trying everything else
besides God, and believe that sickness is something He
cannot reach, but medicine can? as if drugs were superior
to Deity.

The Scripture says, "Ye ask, and receive not, because
ye ask amiss;" and is it not asking amiss to pray for a
proof of divine power, that you have little or no faith in
because you do not understand God, the Principle of
this proof? Prayer will be inaudible, and works more
than words, as we understand God better. The Lord's

1 Prayer, understood in its spiritual sense, and given its
spiritual version, can never be repeated too often for the
3 benefit of all who, having ears, hear and understand.
Metaphysical Science teaches us there is no other Life,
substance, and intelligence but God. How much are you
6 demonstrating of this statement? which to you hath the
most actual substance, — wealth and fame, or Truth and
Love? See to it, O Christian Scientists, ye who have
9 named the name of Christ with a higher meaning, that you
abide by your statements, and abound in Love and Truth,
for unless you do this you are not demonstrating the
12 Science of metaphysical healing. The immeasurable
Life and Love will occupy your affections, come nearer
your hearts and into your homes when you touch but the
15 hem of Truth's garment.

A word about the five personal senses, and we will leave
our abstract subjects for this time. The only evidence we
18 have of sin, sickness, or death is furnished by these senses;
but how can we rely on their testimony when the senses
afford no evidence of Truth? They can neither see, hear,
21 feel, taste, nor smell God; and shall we call that reliable
evidence through which we can gain no understanding of
Truth, Life, and Love? Again, shall we say that God
24 hath created those senses through which it is impossible to
approach Him? Friends, it is of the utmost importance
that we look into these subjects, and gain our evidences of
27 Life from the correct source. Jesus said, "I am the way,
the truth, and the life. No man cometh unto the Father,

but by me," — through the footsteps of Truth. Not by the
senses — the lusts of the flesh, the pride of life, envy,
hypocrisy, or malice, the pleasures or the pains of the
personal senses — does man get nearer his divine nature
and present the image and likeness of God. How, then,
can it be that material man and the personal senses were
created by God? Love makes the spiritual man, lust
makes the material so-called man, and God made all that
was made; therefore the so-called material man and these
personal senses, with all their evidences of sin, sickness,
and death, are but a dream, — they are not the realities of
life; and we shall all learn this as we awake to behold His
likeness.

The allegory of Adam, when spiritually understood,
explains this dream of material life, even the dream of
the "deep sleep" that fell upon Adam when the spiritual
senses were hushed by material sense that before had
claimed audience with a serpent. Sin, sickness, and
death never proceeded from Truth, Life, and Love. Sin,
sickness, and death are error; they are not Truth, and
therefore are not TRUE. Sin is a supposed mental condition; sickness and death are supposed physical ones, but
all appeared through the false supposition of life and intelligence in matter. Sin was first in the allegory, and
sickness and death were produced by sin. Then was not
sin of mental origin, and did not mind originate the delusion? If sickness and death came through mind, so
must they go; and are we not right in ruling them out of

1 mind to destroy their effects upon the body, that both
   mortal mind and mortal body shall yield to the govern-
3 ment of God, immortal Mind? In the words of Paul,
   that "the old man" shall be "put off," mortality shall
   disappear and immortality be brought to light. People are
6 willing to put new wine into old bottles; but if this be
   done, the bottle will break and the wine be spilled.

   There is no connection between Spirit and matter.
9 Spirit never entered and it never escaped from matter;
   good and evil never dwelt together. There is in reality
   but the good: Truth is the real; error, the unreal. We
12 cannot put the new wine into old bottles. If that could be
   done, the world would accept our sentiments; it would willingly adopt the new idea, if that idea could be reconciled
15 with the old belief; it would put the new wine into the
   old bottle if it could prevent its effervescing and keep it
   from popping out until it became popular.

18   The doctrine of atonement never did anything for sickness or claimed to reach that woe; but Jesus' mission
   extended to the sick as much as to the sinner: he estab-
21 lished his Messiahship on the basis that Christ, Truth,
   heals the sick. Pride, appetites, passions, envy, and malice
   will cease to assert their Cæsar sway when metaphysics is
24 understood; and religion at the sick-bed will be no blind
   Samson shorn of his locks. You must admit that what is
   termed death has been produced by a belief alone. The
27 Oxford students proved this: they killed a man by no other
   means than making him believe he was bleeding to death.

A felon was delivered to them for experiment to test the
power of mind over body; and they did test it, and proved
it. They proved it not in part, but as a whole; they
proved that every organ of the system, every function of
the body, is governed directly and entirely by mind, else
those functions could not have been stopped by mind in-
dependently of material conditions. Had they changed
the felon's belief that he was bleeding to death, removed
the bandage from his eyes, and he had seen that a vein had
not been opened, he would have resuscitated. The illusive
origin of disease is not an exception to the origin of all
mortal things. Spirit is causation, and the ancient question, Which is first, the egg or the bird? is answered by
the Scripture, He made "every plant of the field before it
was in the earth."

Heaven's signet is Love. We need it to stamp our religions and to spiritualize thought, motive, and endeavor.
Tireless Being, patient of man's procrastination, affords
him fresh opportunities every hour; but if Science makes
a more spiritual demand, bidding man go up higher, he is
impatient perhaps, or doubts the feasibility of the demand.
But let us work more earnestly in His vineyard, and according to the model on the mount, bearing the cross meekly
along the rugged way, into the wilderness, up the steep
ascent, on to heaven, making our words golden rays in the
sunlight of our deeds; and "these signs shall follow them
that believe; . . . they shall lay hands on the sick, and
they shall recover."

1   The following hymn was sung at the close: —

        "Oh, could we speak the matchless worth,
3   Oh, could we sound the glories forth,
           Which in our Saviour shine,
        We'd soar and touch the heavenly strings,
6   And vie with Gabriel, while he sings,
           In notes almost divine."

THE PEOPLE'S IDEA OF GOD

ITS EFFECT ON

HEALTH AND CHRISTIANITY

A SERMON DELIVERED AT BOSTON

THE

PEOPLE'S IDEA OF GOD

ITS EFFECT ON

HEALTH AND CHRISTIANITY

BY

MARY BAKER EDDY

AUTHOR OF SCIENCE AND HEALTH WITH KEY TO THE
SCRIPTURES

A SERMON DELIVERED AT BOSTON

Registered
U. S. Patent Office

Published by The
Trustees under the Will of Mary Baker G. Eddy
BOSTON, U. S. A.

Authorized Literature of
THE FIRST CHURCH OF CHRIST, SCIENTIST
in Boston, Massachusetts

1 we learn our capabilities for good, which insures man's
continuance and is the true glory of immortality.

3   The improved theory and practice of religion and of
medicine are mainly due to the people's improved views
of the Supreme Being. As the finite sense of Deity, based
6 on material conceptions of spiritual being, yields its grosser
elements, we shall learn what God is, and what God does.
The Hebrew term that gives another letter to the word
9 *God* and makes it *good*, unites Science and Christianity,
whereby we learn that God, good, is universal, and the
divine Principle, — Life, Truth, Love; and this Principle is
12 learned through goodness, and of Mind instead of matter,
of Soul instead of the senses, and by revelation supporting
reason. It is the false conceptions of Spirit, based on the
15 evidences gained from the material senses, that make a
Christian only in theory, shockingly material in practice,
and form its Deity out of the worst human qualities, else
18 of wood or stone.

Such a theory has overturned empires in demoniacal con-
tests over religion. Proportionately as the people's belief
21 of God, in every age, has been dematerialized and unfinited
has their Deity become good; no longer a personal tyrant
or a molten image, but the divine Life, Truth, and Love,
24 — Life without beginning or ending, Truth without a
lapse or error, and Love universal, infinite, eternal. This
more perfect idea, held constantly before the people's
27 mind, must have a benign and elevating influence upon
the character of nations as well as individuals, and will

SERMON

SUBJECT

THE PEOPLE'S IDEA OF GOD

TEXT: *One Lord, one faith, one baptism.* — EPHESIANS iv. 5.

EVERY step of progress is a step more spiritual. The
great element of reform is not born of human wisdom; it draws not its life from human organizations;
rather is it the crumbling away of material elements from
reason, the translation of law back to its original language,
— Mind, and the final unity between man and God.
The footsteps of thought, as they pass from the sensual
side of existence to the reality and Soul of all things, are
slow, portending a long night to the traveller; but the
guardians of the gloom are the angels of His presence, that
impart grandeur to the intellectual wrestling and colli-
sions with old-time faiths, as we drift into more spiritual
latitudes. The beatings of our heart can be heard; but
the ceaseless throbbings and throes of thought are unheard,
as it changes from material to spiritual standpoints. Even
the pangs of death disappear, accordingly as the understanding that we are spiritual beings here reappears, and

lift man ultimately to the understanding that our ideals
form our characters, that as a man "thinketh in his heart,
so is he." The crudest ideals of speculative theology
have made monsters of men; and the ideals of *materia
medica* have made helpless invalids and cripples. The
eternal roasting amidst noxious vapors; the election of the
minority to be saved and the majority to be eternally punished; the wrath of God, to be appeased by the sacrifice
and torture of His favorite Son, — are some of the false
beliefs that have produced sin, sickness, and death; and
then would affirm that these are natural, and that Christianity and Christ-healing are preternatural; yea, that
make a mysterious God and a natural devil.

Let us rejoice that the bow of omnipotence already
spans the moral heavens with light, and that the more
spiritual idea of good and Truth meets the old material
thought like a promise upon the cloud, while it inscribes
on the thoughts of men at this period a more metaphysical
religion founded upon Christian Science. A personal
God is based on finite premises, where thought begins
wrongly to apprehend the infinite, even the quality or the
quantity of eternal good. This limited sense of God as
good limits human thought and action in their goodness,
and assigns them mortal fetters in the outset. It has im-
planted in our religions certain unspiritual shifts, such as
dependence on personal pardon for salvation, rather than
obedience to our Father's demands, whereby we grow out
of sin in the way that our Lord has appointed; namely,

1 by working out our own salvation. It has given to all
systems of *materia medica* nothing but materialism, —
3 more faith in hygiene and drugs than in God. Idolatry
sprang from the belief that God is a form, more than an
infinite and divine Mind; sin, sickness, and death origi-
6 nated in the belief that Spirit materialized into a body,
infinity became finity, or man, and the eternal entered the
temporal. Mythology, or the myth of ologies, said that
9 Life, which is infinite and eternal, could enter finite man
through his nostrils, and matter become intelligent of
good and evil, because a serpent said it. When first good,
12 God, was named a person, and evil another person, the
error that a personal God and a personal devil entered
into partnership and would form a third person, called
15 material man, obtained expression. But these unspiritual and mysterious ideas of God and man are far from
correct.

18   The glorious Godhead is Life, Truth, and Love, and
these three terms for one divine Principle are the three in
one that can be understood, and that find no reflection in
21 sinning, sick, and dying mortals. No miracle of grace can
make a spiritual mind out of beliefs that are as material as
the heathen deities. The pagan priests appointed Apollo
24 and Esculapius the gods of medicine, and they inquired of
these heathen deities what drugs to prescribe. Systems
of religion and of medicine grown out of such false ideals
27 of the Supreme Being cannot heal the sick and cast out
devils, error. Eschewing a materialistic and idolatrous

theory and practice of medicine and religion, the apostle 1
devoutly recommends the more spiritual Christianity, —
"one Lord, one faith, one baptism." The prophets and 3
apostles, whose lives are the embodiment of a living faith,
have not taken away our Lord, that we know not where they
have laid him; they have resurrected a deathless life of 6
love; and into the cold materialisms of dogma and doctrine
we look in vain for their more spiritual ideal, the risen
Christ, whose *materia medica* and theology were one. 9

The ideals of primitive Christianity are nigh, even at
our door. Truth is not lost in the mists of remoteness or
the barbarisms of spiritless codes. The right ideal is not 12
buried, but has risen higher to our mortal sense, and
having overcome death and the grave, wrapped in a pure
winding-sheet, it sitteth beside the sepulchre in angel 15
form, saying unto us, "Life is God; and our ideal of God
has risen above the sod to declare His omnipotence." This
white-robed thought points away from matter and doc- 18
trine, or dogma, to the diviner sense of Life and Love, —
yea, to the Principle that is God, and to the demonstration thereof in healing the sick. Let us then heed this heav- 21
enly visitant, and not entertain the angel unawares.

The ego is not self-existent matter animated by mind,
but in itself is mind; therefore a Truth-filled mind makes 24
a pure Christianity and a healthy mind and body. Oliver
Wendell Holmes said, in a lecture before the Harvard
Medical School: "I firmly believe that if the whole *materia* 27
medica could be sunk to the bottom of the sea, it would be

all the better for mankind and all the worse for the fishes."
Dr. Benjamin Waterhouse writes: "I am sick of learned
quackery." Dr. Abercrombie, Fellow of the Royal College of Physicians in Edinburgh, writes: "Medicine is the science of guessing." Dr. James Johnson, Surgeon Extraordinary to the King, says: "I declare my conscientious belief, founded on long observation and reflection, that if there was not a single physician, surgeon, apothecary, man-midwife, chemist, druggist, or drug on the face of the earth, there would be less sickness and less mortality than now obtains." Voltaire says: "The art of medicine consists in amusing the patient while nature cures the disease."

Believing that man is the victim of his Maker, we naturally fear God more than we love Him; whereas "perfect Love casteth out fear;" but when we learn God aright, we love Him, because He is found altogether lovely. Thus it is that a more spiritual and true ideal of Deity improves the race physically and spiritually. God is no longer a mystery to the Christian Scientist, but a divine Principle, understood in part, because the grand realities of Life and Truth are found destroying sin, sickness, and death; and it should no longer be deemed treason to understand God, when the Scriptures enjoin us to "acquaint now thyself with Him [God], and be at peace;" we should understand something of that great good for which we are to leave all else.

Periods and peoples are characterized by their highest

or their lowest ideals, by their God and their devil. We are   1
all sculptors, working out our own ideals, and leaving the
impress of mind on the body as well as on history and   3
marble, chiselling to higher excellence, or leaving to rot and
ruin the mind's ideals. Recognizing this as we ought, we
shall turn often from marble to model, from matter to   6
Mind, to beautify and exalt our lives.

> "Chisel in hand stood a sculptor-boy,
>   With his marble block before him;   9
> And his face lit up with a smile of joy
>   As an angel dream passed o'er him.
> He carved the dream on that shapeless stone   12
>   With many a sharp incision,
> With heaven's own light the sculptor shone, —
>   He had caught the angel-vision.   15
>
> "Sculptors of life are we as we stand
>   With our lives uncarved before us,
> Waiting the hour when at God's command   18
>   Our life dream passes o'er us.
> If we carve it then on the yielding stone
>   With many a sharp incision,   21
> Its heavenly beauty shall be our own, —
>   Our lives that angel-vision."

To remove those objects of sense called sickness and dis-   24
ease, we must appeal to mind to improve its subjects and
objects of thought, and give to the body those better de-
lineations. Scientific discovery and the inspiration of   27
Truth have taught me that the health and character of
man become more or less perfect as his mind-models are
more or less spiritual. Because God is Spirit, our thoughts   30
must spiritualize to approach Him, and our methods grow
more spiritual to accord with our thoughts. Religion and

1 medicine must be dematerialized to present the right idea
of Truth; then will this idea cast out error and heal the
3 sick. If changeableness that repenteth itself; partiality
that elects some to be saved and others to be lost, or that
answers the prayer of one and not of another; if incom-
6 petency that cannot heal the sick, or lack of love that will
not; if unmercifulness, that for the sins of a few tired
years punishes man eternally, — are our conceptions of
9 Deity, we shall bring out these qualities of character in our
own lives and extend their influence to others.

Judaism, enjoining the limited and definite form of a
12 national religion, was not more the antithesis of Christianity than are our finite and material conceptions of
Deity. Life is God; but we say that Life is carried on
15 through principal processes, and speculate concerning
material forces. Mind is supreme; and yet we make more
of matter, and lean upon it for health and life. Mind,
18 that governs the universe, governs every action of the body
as directly as it moves a planet and controls the muscles
of the arm. God grant that the trembling chords of human
21 hope shall again be swept by the divine *Talitha cumi*,
"Damsel, I say unto thee, arise." Then shall Christian
Science again appear, to light our sepulchres with im-
24 mortality. We thank our Father that to-day the uncre-
mated fossils of material systems, already charred, are
fast fading into ashes; and that man will ere long stop
27 trusting where there is no trust, and gorging his faith with
skill proved a million times unskilful.

Christian Science has one faith, one Lord, one baptism; and this faith builds on Spirit, not matter; and this baptism is the purification of mind, — not an ablution of the body, but tears of repentance, an overflowing love, washing away the motives for sin; yea, it is love leaving self for God. The cool bath may refresh the body, or as compliance with a religious rite may declare one's belief; but it cannot purify his mind, or meet the demands of Love. It is the baptism of Spirit that washes our robes and makes them white in the blood of the Lamb; that bathes us in the life of Truth and the truth of Life. Having one Lord, we shall not be idolaters, dividing our homage and obedience between matter and Spirit; but shall work out our own salvation, after the model of our Father, who never pardons the sin that deserves to be punished and can be destroyed only through suffering.

We ask and receive not, because we "ask amiss;" even dare to invoke the divine aid of Spirit to heal the sick, and then administer drugs with full confidence in their efficacy, showing our greater faith in matter, despite the authority of Jesus that "ye cannot serve two masters."

Silent prayer is a desire, fervent, importunate: here metaphysics is seen to rise above physics, and rest all faith in Spirit, and remove all evidence of any other power than Mind; whereby we learn the great fact that there is no omnipotence, unless omnipotence is the *All*-power. This truth of Deity, understood, destroys discord with the higher and more potent evidences in Christian Science of man's

harmony and immortality. Thought is the essence of an
act, and the stronger element of action; even as steam is
more powerful than water, simply because it is more
ethereal. Essences are refinements that lose some materi-
ality; and as we struggle through the cold night of physics,
matter will become vague, and melt into nothing under the
microscope of Mind.

Massachusetts succored a fugitive slave in 1853, and put
her humane foot on a tyrannical prohibitory law regulating
the practice of·medicine in 1880. It were well if the sister
States had followed her example and sustained as nobly
our constitutional Bill of Rights. Discerning the God-
given rights of man, Paul said, "I was free born." Justice
and truth make man free, injustice and error enslave
him. Mental Science alone grasps the standard of liberty,
and battles for man's whole rights, divine as well as human. It assures us, of a verity, that mortal beliefs, and
not a law of nature, have made men sinning and sick, —
that they alone have fettered free limbs, and marred in
mind the model of man.

We possess our own body, and make it harmonious or
discordant according to the images that thought reflects
upon it. The emancipation of our bodies from sickness
will follow the mind's freedom from sin; and, as St. Paul
admonishes, we should be "waiting for the adoption, to
wit, the redemption of our body." The rights of man were
vindicated but in a single instance when African slavery
was abolished on this continent, yet that hour was a

prophecy of the full liberty of the sons of God as found in
Christian Science. The defenders of the rights of the
colored man were scarcely done with their battles before a
new abolitionist struck the keynote of higher claims, in
which it was found that the feeblest mind, enlightened
and spiritualized, can free its body from disease as well as
sin; and this victory is achieved, not with bayonet and
blood, not by inhuman warfare, but in divine peace.

Above the platform of human rights let us build another
staging for diviner claims, — even the supremacy of Soul
over sense, wherein man cooperates with and is made subject to his Maker. The lame, the blind, the sick, the sensual, are slaves, and their fetters are gnawing away life
and hope; their chains are clasped by the false teachings,
false theories, false fears, that enforce new forms of oppression, and are the modern Pharaohs that hold the children of Israel still in bondage. Mortals, *alias* mortal
minds, make the laws that govern their bodies, as directly
as men pass legislative acts and enact penal codes; while
the body, obedient to the legislation of mind, but ignorant
of the law of belief, calls its own enactments "laws of
matter." The legislators who are greatly responsible for
all the woes of mankind are those leaders of public thought
who are mistaken in their methods of humanity.

The learned quacks of this period "bind heavy bur-
dens," that they themselves will not touch "with one of
their fingers." Scientific guessing conspires unwittingly
against the liberty and lives of men. Should we but

1 hearken to the higher law of God, we should think for one
moment of these divine statutes of God: Let them have
3 "dominion over all the earth." "And if they drink any
deadly thing, it shall not hurt them; they shall lay hands
on the sick, and they shall recover." The only law of sick-
6 ness or death is a law of mortal belief, an infringement
on the merciful and just government of God. When this
great fact is understood, the spurious, imaginary laws of
9 matter — when matter is not a lawgiver — will be dis-
puted and trampled under the feet of Truth. Deal, then,
with this fabulous law as with an inhuman State law; re-
12 peal it in mind, and acknowledge only God in all thy ways,
— "who forgiveth all thine iniquities; who healeth all thy
diseases." Few there be who know what a power mind is
15 to heal when imbued with the spiritual truth that lifts man
above the demands of matter.

As our ideas of Deity advance to truer conceptions,
18 we shall take in the remaining two thirds of God's plan
of redemption, — namely, man's salvation from sickness
and death. Our blessed Master demonstrated this great
21 truth of healing the sick and raising the dead as God's
whole plan, and proved the application of its Principle to
human wants. Having faith in drugs and hygienic drills,
24 we lose faith in omnipotence, and give the healing power
to matter instead of Spirit. As if Deity would not if He
could, or could not if He would, give health to man; when
27 our Father bestows heaven not more willingly than health;
for without health there could be no heaven.

The worshippers of wood and stone have a more mate- 1
rial deity, hence a lower order of humanity, than those
who believe that God is a personal Spirit. But the wor- 3
shippers of a person have a lower order of Christianity than
he who understands that the Divine Being is more than a
person, and can demonstrate in part this great impersonal 6
Life, Truth, and Love, casting out error and healing the
sick. This all-important understanding is gained in
Christian Science, revealing the one God and His all- 9
power and ever-presence, and the brotherhood of man in
unity of Mind and oneness of Principle.

On the startled ear of humanity rings out the iron tread 12
of merciless invaders, putting man to the rack for his
conscience, or forcing from the lips of manhood shameful
confessions, — Galileo kneeling at the feet of priestcraft, 15
and giving the lie to science. But the lofty faith of the
pious Polycarp proved the triumph of mind over the body,
when they threatened to let loose the wild beasts upon him, 18
and he replied: "Let them come; I cannot change at once
from good to bad." Then they bound him to the stake,
set fire to the fagots, and his pure faith went up through 21
the baptism of fire to a higher sense of Life. The infidel
was blind who said, "Christianity is fit only for women and
weak-minded men." But infidels disagree; for Bonaparte 24
said: "Since ever the history of Christianity was written,
the loftiest intellects have had a practical faith in God;"
and Daniel Webster said: "My heart has assured and re- 27
assured me that Christianity must be a divine reality."

1   As our ideas of Deity become more spiritual, we express
them by objects more beautiful. To-day we clothe our
3 thoughts of death with flowers laid upon the bier, and in
our cemeteries with amaranth blossoms, evergreen leaves,
fragrant recesses, cool grottos, smiling fountains, and
6 white monuments. The dismal gray stones of church-
yards have crumbled into decay, as our ideas of Life have
grown more spiritual; and in place of "bat and owl on the
9 bending stones, are wreaths of immortelles, and white
fingers pointing upward." Thus it is that our ideas of
divinity form our models of humanity. O Christian Scien-
12 tist, thou of the church of the new-born; awake to a
higher and holier love for God and man; put on the whole
armor of Truth; rejoice in hope; be patient in tribulation,
15 — that ye may go to the bed of anguish, and look upon this
dream of life in matter, girt with a higher sense of omnipotence; and behold once again the power of divine Life and
18 Love to heal and reinstate man in God's own image and
likeness, having "one Lord, one faith, one baptism."

PULPIT AND PRESS

PULPIT AND PRESS

BY

MARY BAKER EDDY

DISCOVERER AND FOUNDER OF CHRISTIAN SCIENCE
AND AUTHOR OF SCIENCE AND HEALTH WITH
KEY TO THE SCRIPTURES

Registered
U. S. Patent Office

Published by The
Trustees under the Will of Mary Baker G. Eddy
BOSTON, U. S. A.

Authorized Literature of
THE FIRST CHURCH OF CHRIST, SCIENTIST
in Boston, Massachusetts

PRINTED IN THE UNITED STATES OF AMERICA

To

THE DEAR TWO THOUSAND AND SIX HUNDRED CHILDREN

WHOSE CONTRIBUTIONS OF $4,460* WERE DEVOTED
TO THE MOTHER'S ROOM IN THE FIRST CHURCH
OF CHRIST, SCIENTIST, BOSTON, THIS UNIQUE
BOOK IS TENDERLY DEDICATED BY

MARY BAKER EDDY

* See footnote on page nine.

PREFACE

THIS volume contains scintillations from press and 1
pulpit — utterances which epitomize the story of the
birth of Christian Science, in 1866, and its progress 3
during the ensuing thirty years. Three quarters of a
century hence, when the children of to-day are the elders
of the twentieth century, it will be interesting to have 6
not only a record of the inclination given their own
thoughts in the latter half of the nineteenth century,
but also a registry of the rise of the mercury in the glass 9
of the world's opinion.

It will then be instructive to turn backward the tele-
scope of that advanced age, with its lenses of more 12
spiritual mentality, indicating the gain of intellectual
momentum, on the early footsteps of Christian Science
as planted in the pathway of this generation; to note 15
the impetus thereby given to Christianity; to con the
facts surrounding the cradle of this grand verity — that
the sick are healed and sinners saved, not by matter, but 18
by Mind; and to scan further the features of the vast
problem of eternal life, as expressed in the absolute
power of Truth and the actual bliss of man's existence 21
in Science.

MARY BAKER EDDY

February, 1895

24

PREFACE

MARY BAKER EDDY.

CONTENTS

CLIPPINGS FROM NEWSPAPERS

PULPIT AND PRESS

DEDICATORY SERMON

By Rev. Mary Baker Eddy

First Pastor of The First Church of Christ, Scientist, Boston, Mass.
Delivered January 6, 1895

TEXT: *They shall be abundantly satisfied with the fatness of Thy* 1
house; and Thou shalt make them drink of the river of Thy pleasures.
— PSALMS xxxvi. 8.   3

A NEW year is a nursling, a babe of time, a prophecy
and promise clad in white raiment, kissed — and
encumbered with greetings — redolent with grief and   6
gratitude.

An old year is time's adult, and 1893 was a distinguished
character, notable for good and evil. Time past and time   9
present, both, may pain us, but time *improved* is elo-
quent in God's praise. For due refreshment garner the
memory of 1894; for if wiser by reason of its large lessons, 12
and records deeply engraven, great is the value thereof.

Pass on, returnless year!
The path behind thee is with glory crowned;   15
This spot whereon thou troddest was holy ground;
Pass proudly to thy bier!

To-day, being with you in spirit, what need that I should   18
be present *in propria persona?* Were I present, methinks

1

I should be much like the Queen of Sheba, when she saw the house Solomon had erected. In the expressive language of Holy Writ, "There was no more spirit in her;" and she said, "Behold, the half was not told me: thy wisdom and prosperity exceedeth the fame which I heard." Both without and within, the spirit of beauty dominates The Mother Church, from its mosaic flooring to the soft shimmer of its starlit dome.

Nevertheless, there is a thought higher and deeper than the edifice. Material light and shade are temporal, not eternal. Turning the attention from sublunary views, however enchanting, think for a moment with me of the house wherewith "they shall be abundantly satisfied," — even the "house not made with hands, eternal in the heavens." With the mind's eye glance at the direful scenes of the war between China and Japan. Imagine yourselves in a poorly barricaded fort, fiercely besieged by the enemy. Would you rush forth single-handed to combat the foe? Nay, would you not rather strengthen your citadel by every means in your power, and remain within the walls for its defense? Likewise should we do as metaphysicians and Christian Scientists. The real house in which "we live, and move, and have our being" is Spirit, God, the eternal harmony of infinite Soul. The enemy we confront would overthrow this sublime fortress, and it behooves us to defend our heritage.

How can we do this Christianly scientific work? By intrenching ourselves in the knowledge that our true temple is no human fabrication, but the superstructure of Truth, reared on the foundation of Love, and pinnacled

in Life. Such being its nature, how can our godly temple
possibly be demolished, or even disturbed? Can eternity
end? Can Life die? Can Truth be uncertain? Can
Love be less than boundless? Referring to this temple,
our Master said: "Destroy this temple, and in three days
I will raise it up." He also said: "The kingdom of God
is within you." Know, then, that you possess sovereign
power to think and act rightly, and that nothing can dis-
possess you of this heritage and trespass on Love. If you
maintain this position, who or what can cause you to sin
or suffer? Our surety is in our confidence that we are
indeed dwellers in Truth and Love, man's eternal mansion.
Such a heavenly assurance ends all warfare, and bids tumult cease, for the good fight we have waged is over, and
divine Love gives us the true sense of victory. "They
shall be abundantly satisfied with the fatness of Thy house;
and Thou shalt make them drink of the river of Thy
pleasures." No longer are we of the church militant, but
of the church triumphant; and with Job of old we ex-
claim, "Yet in my flesh shall I see God." The river of
His pleasures is a tributary of divine Love, whose living
waters have their source in God, and flow into everlasting
Life. We drink of this river when all human desires are
quenched, satisfied with what is pleasing to the divine
Mind.

Perchance some one of you may say, "The evidence of
spiritual verity in me is so small that I am afraid. I feel
so far from victory over the flesh that to reach out for a
present realization of my hope savors of temerity. Because of my own unfitness for such a spiritual animus my

strength is naught and my faith fails." O thou "weak and infirm of purpose." Jesus said, "Be not afraid"!

"What if the little rain should say,
'So small a drop as I
Can ne'er refresh a drooping earth,
I'll tarry in the sky.'"

Is not a man metaphysically and mathematically number one, a unit, and therefore whole number, governed and protected by his divine Principle, God? You have simply to preserve a scientific, positive sense of unity with your divine source, and daily demonstrate this. Then you will find that one is as important a factor as duodecillions in being and doing right, and thus demonstrating deific Principle. A dewdrop reflects the sun. Each of Christ's little ones reflects the infinite One, and therefore is the seer's declaration true, that "one on God's side is a majority."

A single drop of water may help to hide the stars, or crown the tree with blossoms.

Who lives in good, lives also in God, — lives in all Life, through all space. His is an individual kingdom, his diadem a crown of crowns. His existence is deathless, forever unfolding its eternal Principle. Wait patiently on illimitable Love, the lord and giver of Life. *Reflect this Life*, and with it cometh the full power of being. "They shall be abundantly satisfied with the fatness of Thy house."

In 1893 the World's Parliament of Religions, held in Chicago, used, in all its public sessions, my form of prayer since 1866; and one of the very clergymen who had publicly proclaimed me "the prayerless Mrs. Eddy," offered his audible adoration in the words I use, besides listening to an address on Christian Science from my pen, read by Judge S. J. Hanna, in that unique assembly.

When the light of one friendship after another passes from earth to heaven, we kindle in place thereof the glow of some deathless reality. Memory, faithful to goodness, holds in her secret chambers those characters of holiest sort, bravest to endure, firmest to suffer, soonest to renounce. Such was the founder of the Concord School of Philosophy — the late A. Bronson Alcott.

After the publication of "Science and Health with Key to the Scriptures," his athletic mind, scholarly and serene, was the first to bedew my hope with a drop of humanity. When the press and pulpit cannonaded this book, he introduced himself to its author by saying, "I have come to comfort you." Then eloquently paraphrasing it, and prophesying its prosperity, his conversation with a beauty all its own reassured me. *That prophecy is fulfilled.*

This book, in 1895, is in its ninety-first edition of one thousand copies. It is in the public libraries of the principal cities, colleges, and universities of America; also the same in Great Britain, France, Germany, Russia, Italy, Greece, Japan, India, and China; in the Oxford University and the Victoria Institute, England; in the Academy of Greece, and the Vatican at Rome.

This book is the leaven fermenting religion; it is palpably working in the sermons, Sunday Schools, and literature of our and other lands. This spiritual chemi-

1 calization is the upheaval produced when Truth is neutral-
izing error and impurities are passing off. And it will
3 continue till the antithesis of Christianity, engendering the
limited forms of a national or tyrannical religion, yields to
the church established by the Nazarene Prophet and main-
6 tained on the spiritual foundation of Christ's healing.

Good, the Anglo-Saxon term for God, unites Science to
Christianity. It presents to the understanding, not matter,
9 but Mind; not the deified drug, but the goodness of God —
healing and saving mankind.

The author of "Marriage of the Lamb," who made the
12 mistake of thinking she caught her notions from my book,
wrote to me in 1894, "Six months ago your book, Science
and Health, was put into my hands. I had not read three
15 pages before I realized I had found that for which I had
hungered since girlhood, and was healed instantaneously
of an ailment of seven years' standing. I cast from me the
18 false remedy I had vainly used, and turned to the 'great
Physician.' I went with my husband, a missionary to
China, in 1884. He went out under the auspices of the
21 Methodist Episcopal Church. I feel the truth is leading
us to return to Japan."

Another brilliant enunciator, seeker, and servant of
24 Truth, the Rev. William R. Alger of Boston, signalled
me kindly as my lone bark rose and fell and rode the rough
sea. At a *conversazione* in Boston, he said, "You may
27 find in Mrs. Eddy's metaphysical teachings more than is
dreamt of in your philosophy."

Also that renowned apostle of anti-slavery, Wendell
30 Phillips, the native course of whose mind never swerved

from the chariot-paths of justice, speaking of my work, said: "Had I young blood in my veins, I would help that woman."

I love Boston, and especially the laws of the State whereof this city is the capital. To-day, as of yore, her laws have befriended progress.

Yet when I recall the past, — how the gospel of healing was simultaneously praised and persecuted in Boston, — and remember also that God is just, I wonder whether, were our dear Master in our New England metropolis at this hour, he would not weep over it, as he wept over Jerusalem! O ye tears! Not in vain did ye flow. Those sacred drops were but enshrined for future use, and God has now unsealed their receptacle with His outstretched arm. Those crystal globes made morals for mankind. They will rise with joy, and with power to wash away, in floods of forgiveness, every crime, even when mistakenly committed in the name of religion.

An unjust, unmerciful, and oppressive priesthood must perish, for false prophets in the present as in the past stumble onward to their doom; while their tabernacles crumble with dry rot. "God is not mocked," and "the word of the Lord endureth forever."

I have ordained the Bible and the Christian Science textbook, "Science and Health with Key to the Scriptures," as pastor of The First Church of Christ, Scientist, in Boston, — so long as this church is satisfied with this pastor. This is my first ordination. "They shall be abundantly satisfied with the fatness of Thy house; and Thou shalt make them drink of the river of Thy pleasures."

All praise to the press of America's Athens, — and
throughout our land the press has spoken out historically,
impartially. Like the winds telling tales through the
leaves of an ancient oak, unfallen, may our church chimes
repeat my thanks to the press.

Notwithstanding the perplexed condition of our nation's finances, the want and woe with millions of dollars
unemployed in our money centres, the Christian Scientists,
within fourteen months, responded to the call for this
church with $191,012. Not a mortgage was given nor a
loan solicited, and the donors all touchingly told their
privileged joy at helping to build The Mother Church.
There was no urging, begging, or borrowing; only the
need made known, and forth came the money, or dia-
monds, which served to erect this "miracle in stone."

Even the children vied with their parents to meet the
demand. Little hands, never before devoted to menial
services, shoveled snow, and babes gave kisses to earn a
few pence toward this consummation. Some of these
lambs my prayers had christened, but Christ will rechristen
them with his own new name. "Out of the mouths of
babes and sucklings Thou hast perfected praise." The
resident youthful workers were called "Busy Bees."

Sweet society, precious children, your loving hearts and
deft fingers distilled the nectar and painted the finest
flowers in the fabric of this history, — even its centre-piece,
— Mother's Room in The First Church of Christ, Scientist, in Boston. The children are destined to witness
results which will eclipse Oriental dreams. They belong
to the twentieth century. By juvenile aid, into the build-

ing fund have come $4,460.* Ah, children, you are the
bulwarks of freedom, the cement of society, the hope of
our race!

Brothers of the Christian Science Board of Directors,
when your tireless tasks are done — well done — no Delphian lyre could break the full chords of such a rest. May
the altar you have built never be shattered in our hearts,
but justice, mercy, and love kindle perpetually its fires.

It was well that the brother whose appliances warm
this house, warmed also our perishless hope, and nerved
its grand fulfilment. Woman, true to her instinct, came
to the rescue as sunshine from the clouds; so, when man
quibbled over an architectural exigency, a woman climbed
with feet and hands to the top of the tower, and helped
settle the subject.

After the loss of our late lamented pastor, Rev. D. A.
Easton, the church services were maintained by excellent
sermons from the editor of *The Christian Science Journal*
(who, with his better half, is a very whole man), together
with the Sunday School giving this flock "drink from the
river of His pleasures." O glorious hope and blessed assurance, "it is your Father's good pleasure to give you the
kingdom." Christians rejoice in secret, they have a bounty
hidden from the world. Self-forgetfulness, purity, and
love are treasures untold — constant prayers, prophecies,
and anointings. Practice, not profession, — goodness, not
doctrines, — spiritual understanding, not mere belief,
gain the ear and right hand of omnipotence, and call down
blessings infinite. "Faith without works is dead." The
foundation of enlightened faith is Christ's teachings and

* This sum was increased to $5,568.51 by contributions which reached the Treasurer after the Dedicatory Services.

1 *practice.* It was our Master's self-immolation, his life-
giving love, healing both mind and body, that raised the
3 deadened conscience, paralyzed by inactive faith, to a
quickened sense of mortal's necessities, — and God's
power and purpose to supply them. It was, in the words
6 of the Psalmist, He "who forgiveth all thine iniquities;
who healeth all thy diseases."

Rome's fallen fanes and silent Aventine is glory's tomb;
9 her pomp and power lie low in dust. Our land, more
favored, had its Pilgrim Fathers. On shores of solitude,
at Plymouth Rock, they planted a nation's heart, — the
12 rights of conscience, imperishable glory. No dream of
avarice or ambition broke their exalted purpose, theirs
was the wish to reign in hope's reality — the realm of
15 Love.

Christian Scientists, you have planted your standard
on the rock of Christ, the true, the spiritual idea, — the
18 chief corner-stone in the house of our God. And our
Master said: "The stone which the builders rejected, the
same is become the head of the corner." If you are less
21 appreciated to-day than your forefathers, wait — for if
you are as devout as they, and more scientific, as progress
certainly demands, your plant is immortal. Let us rejoice
24 that chill vicissitudes have not withheld the timely shelter
of this house, which descended like day-spring from on
high.

27   Divine presence, breathe Thou Thy blessing on every
heart in this house. Speak out, O soul! This is the new-
born of Spirit, this is His redeemed; this, His beloved.
30 May the kingdom of God within you, — with you alway, —

reascending, bear you outward, upward, heavenward. 1
May the sweet song of silver-throated singers, making
melody more real, and the organ's voice, as the sound of 3
many waters, and the Word spoken in this sacred temple
dedicated to the ever-present God — mingle with the joy
of angels and rehearse your hearts' holy intents. May all 6
whose means, energies, and prayers helped erect The
Mother Church, find within it home, and *heaven*.

CHRISTIAN SCIENCE TEXTBOOK

1 The following selections from "Science and Health
   with Key to the Scriptures," pages 568–571, were read
3 from the platform. The impressive stillness of the audience indicated close attention.

   Revelation xii. 10–12. And I heard a loud voice saying in
6 heaven, Now is come salvation, and strength, and the kingdom of our God, and the power of His Christ: for the accuser
   of our brethren is cast down, which accused them before our
9 God day and night. And they overcame him by the blood
   of the Lamb, and by the word of their testimony; and they
   loved not their lives unto the death. Therefore rejoice, ye
12 heavens, and ye that dwell in them. Woe to the inhabiters
   of the earth and of the sea! for the devil is come down unto
   you, having great wrath, because he knoweth that he hath
15 but a short time.

   For victory over a single sin, we give thanks and mag-
   nify the Lord of Hosts. What shall we say of the mighty
18 conquest over all sin? A louder song, sweeter than has
   ever before reached high heaven, now rises clearer and
   nearer to the great heart of Christ; for the accuser is not
21 there, and Love sends forth her primal and everlasting
   strain. Self-abnegation, by which we lay down all for
   Truth, or Christ, in our warfare against error, is a rule in
24 Christian Science. This rule clearly interprets God as

12

divine Principle, — as Life, represented by the Father; as Truth, represented by the Son; as Love, represented by the Mother. Every mortal at some period, here or hereafter, must grapple with and overcome the mortal belief in a power opposed to God.

The Scripture, "Thou hast been faithful over a few things, I will make thee ruler over many," is literally fulfilled, when we are conscious of the supremacy of Truth, by which the nothingness of error is seen; and we know that the nothingness of error is in proportion to its wickedness. He that touches the hem of Christ's robe and masters his mortal beliefs, animality, and hate, rejoices in the proof of healing, — in a sweet and certain sense that God is Love. Alas for those who break faith with divine Science and fail to strangle the serpent of sin as well as of sickness! They are dwellers still in the deep darkness of belief. They are in the surging sea of error, not struggling to lift their heads above the drowning wave.

What must the end be? They must eventually expiate their sin through suffering. The sin, which one has made his bosom companion, comes back to him at last with accelerated force, for the devil knoweth his time is short. Here the Scriptures declare that evil is temporal, not eternal. The dragon is at last stung to death by his own malice; but how many periods of torture it may take to remove all sin, must depend upon sin's obduracy.

Revelation xii. 13. And when the dragon saw that he was cast unto the earth, he persecuted the woman which brought forth the man child.

1 The march of mind and of honest investigation will
bring the hour when the people will chain, with fetters of
3 some sort, the growing occultism of this period. The
present apathy as to the tendency of certain active yet un-
seen mental agencies will finally be shocked into another
6 extreme mortal mood, — into human indignation; for
one extreme follows another.

Revelation xii. 15, 16. And the serpent cast out of his
9 mouth water as a flood, after the woman, that he might
cause her to be carried away of the flood. And the earth
helped the woman, and the earth opened her mouth, and
12 swallowed up the flood which the dragon cast out of his
mouth.

Millions of unprejudiced minds — simple seekers for
15 Truth, weary wanderers, athirst in the desert — are waiting and watching for rest and drink. Give them a cup of
cold water in Christ's name, and never fear the conse-
18 quences. What if the old dragon should send forth a new
flood to drown the Christ-idea? He can neither drown
your voice with its roar, nor again sink the world into the
21 deep waters of chaos and old night. In this age the earth
will help the woman; the spiritual idea will be understood.
Those ready for the blessing you impart will give thanks.
24 The waters will be pacified, and Christ will command the
wave.

When God heals the sick or the sinning, they should
27 know the great benefit which Mind has wrought. They
should also know the great delusion of mortal mind, when
it makes them sick or sinful. Many are willing to open

the eyes of the people to the power of good resident in divine Mind, but they are not so willing to point out the evil in human thought, and expose evil's hidden mental ways of accomplishing iniquity.

Why this backwardness, since exposure is necessary to ensure the avoidance of the evil? Because people like you better when you tell them their virtues than when you tell them their vices. It requires the spirit of our blessed Master to tell a man his faults, and so risk human displeasure for the sake of doing right and benefiting our race. Who is telling mankind of the foe in ambush? Is the informer one who sees the foe? If so, listen and be wise. Escape from evil, and designate those as unfaithful stewards who have seen the danger and yet have given no warning.

At all times and under all circumstances, overcome evil with good. Know thyself, and God will supply the wisdom and the occasion for a victory over evil. Clad in the panoply of Love, human hatred cannot reach you. The cement of a higher humanity will unite all interests in the one divinity.

HYMNS

By Rev. Mary Baker Eddy

1 [Set to the Church Chimes and Sung on This Occasion]

Laying the Corner-stone

3 *Laus Deo*, it is done!
Rolled away from loving heart
    Is a stone.
6 Joyous, risen, we depart
    Having one.

Laus Deo, — on this rock
9 (Heaven chiselled squarely good)
    Stands His church, —
God is Love, and understood
12   By His flock.

Laus Deo, night starlit
Slumbers not in God's embrace;
15   Then, O man!
Like this stone, be in thy place;
    Stand, not sit.

18 Cold, silent, stately stone,
Dirge and song and shoutings low,
    In thy heart
21 Dwell serene, — and sorrow? No,
    It has none,
    Laus Deo!

16

"Feed My Sheep"

Shepherd, show me how to go
  O'er the hillside steep,
How to gather, how to sow, —
  How to feed Thy sheep;
I will listen for Thy voice,
  Lest my footsteps stray;
I will follow and rejoice
  All the rugged way.

Thou wilt bind the stubborn will,
  Wound the callous breast,
Make self-righteousness be still,
  Break earth's stupid rest.
Strangers on a barren shore,
  Lab'ring long and lone —
We would enter by the door,
  And Thou know'st Thine own.

So, when day grows dark and cold,
  Tear or triumph harms,
Lead Thy lambkins to the fold,
  Take them in Thine arms;
Feed the hungry, heal the heart,
  Till the morning's beam;
White as wool, ere they depart —
  Shepherd, wash them clean.

CHRIST MY REFUGE

O'er waiting harpstrings of the mind
    There sweeps a strain,
Low, sad, and sweet, whose measures bind
    The power of pain.

And wake a white-winged angel throng
    Of thoughts, illumed
By faith, and breathed in raptured song,
    With love perfumed.

Then his unveiled, sweet mercies show
    Life's burdens light.
I kiss the cross, and wake to know
    A world more bright.

And o'er earth's troubled, angry sea
    I see Christ walk,
And come to me, and tenderly,
    Divinely talk.

Thus Truth engrounds me on the rock,
    Upon Life's shore;
'Gainst which the winds and waves can shock,
    Oh, nevermore!

From tired joy and grief afar,
    And nearer Thee, —
Father, where Thine own children are,
    I love to be.

My prayer, some daily good to do   1
    To Thine, for Thee;
An offering pure of Love, whereto   3
    God leadeth me.

NOTE

By Rev. Mary Baker Eddy

1 The land whereon stands The First Church of Christ,
Scientist, in Boston, was first purchased by the church
3 and society. Owing to a heavy loss, they were unable to
pay the mortgage; therefore I paid it, and through trustees
gave back the land to the church.

6 In 1892 I had to recover the land from the trustees, re-
organize the church, and reobtain its charter — not, however, through the State Commissioner, who refused to
9 grant it, but by means of a statute of the State, and through
Directors regive the land to the church. In 1895 I reconstructed my original system of ministry and church gov-
12 ernment. Thus committed to the providence of God, the
prosperity of this church is unsurpassed.

From first to last The Mother Church seemed type and
15 shadow of the warfare between the flesh and Spirit, even
that shadow whose substance is the divine Spirit, im-
peratively propelling the greatest moral, physical, civil,
18 and religious reform ever known on earth. In the words
of the prophet: "The shadow of a great rock in a weary
land."

21 This church was dedicated on January 6, anciently one
of the many dates selected and observed in the East as the
day of the birth and baptism of our master Metaphysician,
24 Jesus of Nazareth.

Christian Scientists, their children and grandchildren
to the latest generations, inevitably love one another with
that love wherewith Christ loveth us; a love unselfish,
unambitious, impartial, universal, — that loves only because it *is* Love. Moreover, they love their enemies, even
those that hate them. This we all must do to be Christian
Scientists in spirit and in truth. I long, and live, to see
this love demonstrated. I am seeking and praying for it
to inhabit my own heart and to be made manifest in my
life. Who will unite with me in this pure purpose, and
faithfully struggle till it be accomplished? Let this be our
Christian endeavor society, which Christ organizes and
blesses.

While we entertain due respect and fellowship for what
is good and doing good in all denominations of religion,
and shun whatever would isolate us from a true sense of
goodness in others, we cannot serve mammon.

Christian Scientists are really united to only that which
is Christlike, but they are not indifferent to the welfare of
any one. To perpetuate a cold distance between our denomination and other sects, and close the door on church
or individuals — however much this is done to us — is
not Christian Science. Go not into the way of the un-
christly, but wheresoever you recognize a clear expression
of God's likeness, there abide in confidence and hope.

Our unity with churches of other denominations must
rest on the spirit of Christ calling us together. It cannot
come from any other source. Popularity, self-aggrandize-
ment, aught that can darken in any degree our spirituality,
must be set aside. Only what feeds and fills the sentiment

1 with unworldliness, can give peace and good will towards
men.

3   All Christian churches have one bond of unity, one
nucleus or point of convergence, one prayer, — the Lord's
Prayer. It is matter for rejoicing that we unite in love,
6 and in this sacred petition with every praying assembly
on earth, — "Thy kingdom come. Thy will be done in
earth, as it is in heaven."

9   If the lives of Christian Scientists attest their fidelity
to Truth, I predict that in the twentieth century every
Christian church in our land, and a few in far-off lands,
12 will approximate the understanding of Christian Science
sufficiently to heal the sick in his name. Christ will give
to Christianity his new name, and Christendom will be
15 classified as Christian Scientists.

When the doctrinal barriers between the churches are
broken, and the bonds of peace are cemented by spiritual
18 understanding and Love, there will be unity of spirit, and
the healing power of Christ will prevail. Then shall Zion
have put on her most beautiful garments, and her waste
21 places budded and blossomed as the rose.

CLIPPINGS FROM NEWSPAPERS

[*Daily Inter-Ocean*, Chicago, December 31, 1894] 1

MARY BAKER EDDY

COMPLETION OF THE FIRST CHURCH OF CHRIST, SCIENTIST, BOSTON 3
— "OUR PRAYER IN STONE" — DESCRIPTION OF THE MOST
UNIQUE STRUCTURE IN ANY CITY — A BEAUTIFUL TEMPLE
AND ITS FURNISHINGS — MRS. EDDY'S WORK AND HER IN- 6
FLUENCE

Boston, Mass., December 28. — *Special Correspondence.* — The "great awakening" of the time of Jonathan 9
Edwards has been paralleled during the last decade by a
wave of idealism that has swept over the country, mani-
festing itself under several different aspects and under 12
various names, but each having the common identity of
spiritual demand. This movement, under the guise of
Christian Science, and ingenuously calling out a closer 15
inquiry into Oriental philosophy, prefigures itself to us
as one of the most potent factors in the social evolution
of the last quarter of the nineteenth century. History 18
shows the curious fact that the closing years of every century are years of more intense life, manifested in unrest
or in aspiration, and scholars of special research, like 21
Prof. Max Muller, assert that the end of a cycle, as is the
latter part of the present century, is marked by peculiar
intimations of man's immortal life. 24

23

1   The completion of the first Christian Science church erected in Boston strikes a keynote of definite attention.
3 This church is in the fashionable Back Bay, between Commonwealth and Huntington Avenues. It is one of the most beautiful, and is certainly the most unique struc-
6 ture in any city. The First Church of Christ, Scientist, as it is officially called, is termed by its Founder, "Our prayer in stone." It is located at the intersection of Nor-
9 way and Falmouth Streets, on a triangular plot of ground, the design a Romanesque tower with a circular front and an octagonal form, accented by stone porticos and turreted
12 corners. On the front is a marble tablet, with the following inscription carved in bold relief: —

   "The First Church of Christ, Scientist, erected Anno
15 Domini 1894. A testimonial to our beloved teacher, the Rev. Mary Baker Eddy, Discoverer and Founder of Christian Science; author of "Science and Health
18 with Key to the Scriptures;" president of the Massachusetts Metaphysical College, and the first pastor of this denomination."

21   THE CHURCH EDIFICE

   The church is built of Concord granite in light gray, with trimmings of the pink granite of New Hampshire,
24 Mrs. Eddy's native State. The architecture is Romanesque throughout. The tower is one hundred and twenty feet in height and twenty-one and one half feet square. The en-
27 trances are of marble, with doors of antique oak richly carved. The windows of stained glass are very rich in

pictorial effect. The lighting and cooling of the church — for cooling is a recognized feature as well as heating — are done by electricity, and the heat generated by two large boilers in the basement is distributed by the four systems with motor electric power. The partitions are of iron; the floors of marble in mosaic work, and the edifice is therefore as literally fire-proof as is conceivable. The principal features are the auditorium, seating eleven hundred people and capable of holding fifteen hundred; the "Mother's Room," designed for the exclusive use of Mrs. Eddy; the "directors' room," and the vestry. The girders are all of iron, the roof is of terra cotta tiles, the galleries are in plaster relief, the window frames are of iron, coated with plaster; the staircases are of iron, with marble stairs of rose pink, and marble approaches.

The vestibule is a fitting entrance to this magnificent temple. In the ceiling is a sunburst with a seven-pointed star, which illuminates it. From this are the entrances leading to the auditorium, the "Mother's Room," and the directors' room.

The auditorium is seated with pews of curly birch, upholstered in old rose plush. The floor is in white Italian mosaic, with frieze of the old rose, and the wainscoting repeats the same tints. The base and cap are of pink Tennessee marble. On the walls are bracketed oxidized silver lamps of Roman design, and there are frequent illuminated texts from the Bible and from Mrs. Eddy's "Science and Health with Key to the Scriptures" impanelled. A sunburst in the centre of the ceiling takes the place of chandeliers. There is a disc of cut glass in

1 decorative designs, covering one hundred and forty-four
electric lights in the form of a star, which is twenty-one
3 inches from point to point, the centre being of pure white
light, and each ray under prisms which reflect the rainbow
tints. The galleries are richly panelled in relief work.
6 The organ and choir gallery is spacious and rich beyond
the power of words to depict. The platform — corre-
sponding to the chancel of an Episcopal church — is a
9 mosaic work, with richly carved seats following the sweep
of its curve, with a lamp stand of the Renaissance period
on either end, bearing six richly wrought oxidized silver
12 lamps, eight feet in height. The great organ comes from
Detroit. It is one of vast compass, with Æolian attachment, and cost eleven thousand dollars. It is the gift of
15 a single individual — a votive offering of gratitude for the
healing of the wife of the donor.

The chime of bells includes fifteen, of fine range and
18 perfect tone.

THE "MOTHER'S ROOM"

The "Mother's Room" is approached by an entrance of
21 Italian marble, and over the door, in large golden letters on
a marble tablet, is the word "Love." In this room the
mosaic marble floor of white has a Romanesque border and
24 is decorated with sprays of fig leaves bearing fruit. The
room is toned in pale green with relief in old rose. The
mantel is of onyx and gold. Before the great bay window
27 hangs an Athenian lamp over two hundred years old,
which will be kept always burning day and night. Lead-

ing off the "Mother's Room" are toilet apartments, with   1
full-length French mirrors and every convenience.

The directors' room is very beautiful in marble ap-   3
proaches and rich carving, and off this is a vault for the
safe preservation of papers.

The vestry seats eight hundred people, and opening from   6
it are three large class-rooms and the pastor's study.

The windows are a remarkable feature of this temple.
There are no "memorial" windows; the entire church is a   9
testimonial, not a memorial — a point that the members
strongly insist upon.

In the auditorium are two rose windows — one repre-   12
senting the heavenly city which "cometh down from God
out of heaven," with six small windows beneath, emblematic of the six water-pots referred to in John ii. 6. The   15
other rose window represents the raising of the daughter
of Jairus. Beneath are two small windows bearing palms
of victory, and others with lamps, typical of Science and   18
Health.

Another great window tells its pictorial story of the four
Marys — the mother of Jesus, Mary anointing the head of   21
Jesus, Mary washing the feet of Jesus, Mary at the resur-
rection; and the woman spoken of in the Apocalypse,
chapter 12, God-crowned.   24

One more window in the auditorium represents the
raising of Lazarus.

In the gallery are windows representing John on the   27
Isle of Patmos, and others of pictorial significance. In
the "Mother's Room" the windows are of still more unique
interest. A large bay window, composed of three separate   30

1 panels, is designed to be wholly typical of the work of Mrs.
Eddy. The central panel represents her in solitude and
3 meditation, searching the Scriptures by the light of a single
candle, while the star of Bethlehem shines down from above.
Above this is a panel containing the Christian Science seal,
6 and other panels are decorated with emblematic designs,
with the legends, "Heal the Sick," "Raise the Dead,"
"Cleanse the Lepers," and "Cast out Demons."

9 The cross and the crown and the star are presented in
appropriate decorative effect. The cost of this church is
two hundred and twenty-one thousand dollars, exclusive
12 of the land — a gift from Mrs. Eddy — which is valued
at some forty thousand dollars.

THE ORDER OF SERVICE

15 The order of service in the Christian Science Church
does not differ widely from that of any other sect, save that
its service includes the use of Mrs. Eddy's book, entitled
18 "Science and Health with Key to the Scriptures," in perhaps equal measure to its use of the Bible. The reading
is from the two alternately; the singing is from a compila-
21 tion called the "Christian Science Hymnal," but its songs
are for the most part those devotional hymns from Herbert,
Faber, Robertson, Wesley, Bowring, and other recog-
24 nized devotional poets, with selections from Whittier and
Lowell, as are found in the hymn-books of the Unitarian
churches. For the past year or two Judge Hanna, for-
27 merly of Chicago, has filled the office of pastor to the
church in this city, which held its meetings in Chickering

Hall, and later in Copley Hall, in the new Grundmann
Studio Building on Copley Square. Preceding Judge
Hanna were Rev. D. A. Easton and Rev. L. P. Norcross,
both of whom had formerly been Congregational clergymen. The organizer and first pastor of the church here
was Mrs. Eddy herself, of whose work I shall venture to
speak, a little later, in this article.

Last Sunday I gave myself the pleasure of attending the
service held in Copley Hall. The spacious apartment was
thronged with a congregation whose remarkable earnestness impressed the observer. There was no straggling
of late-comers. Before the appointed hour every seat in the
hall was filled and a large number of chairs pressed into
service for the overflowing throng. The music was spirited,
and the selections from the Bible and from Science and
Health were finely read by Judge Hanna. Then came his
sermon, which dealt directly with the command of Christ
to "heal the sick, raise the dead, cleanse the lepers, cast
out demons." In his admirable discourse Judge Hanna
said that while all these injunctions could, under certain
conditions, be interpreted and fulfilled literally, the
special lesson was to be taken spiritually — to cleanse the
leprosy of sin, to cast out the demons of evil thought.
The discourse was able, and helpful in its suggestive
interpretation.

THE CHURCH MEMBERS

Later I was told that almost the entire congregation was
composed of persons who had either been themselves, or

1 had seen members of their own families, healed by Christian Science treatment; and I was further told that once
3 when a Boston clergyman remonstrated with Judge Hanna for enticing a separate congregation rather than offering their strength to unite with churches already established —
6 I was told he replied that the Christian Science Church did not recruit itself from other churches, but from the graveyards! The church numbers now four thousand members;
9 but this estimate, as I understand, is not limited to the Boston adherents, but includes those all over the country. The ceremonial of uniting is to sign a brief "confession of
12 faith," written by Mrs. Eddy, and to unite in communion, which is not celebrated by outward symbols of bread and wine, but by uniting in silent prayer.

15   The "confession of faith" includes the declaration that the Scriptures are the guide to eternal Life; that there is a Supreme Being, and His Son, and the Holy Ghost, and
18 that man is made in His image. It affirms the atonement; it recognizes Jesus as the teacher and guide to salvation; the forgiveness of sin by God, and affirms the power of
21 Truth over error, and the need of living faith at the moment to realize the possibilities of the divine Life. The entire membership of Christian Scientists throughout
24 the world now exceeds two hundred thousand people. The church in Boston was organized by Mrs. Eddy, and the first meeting held on April 19, 1879. It opened with
27 twenty-six members, and within fifteen years it has grown to its present impressive proportions, and has now its own magnificent church building, costing over two hundred
30 thousand dollars, and entirely paid for when its consecra-

tion service on January 6 shall be celebrated. This is certainly a very remarkable retrospect.

Rev. Mary Baker Eddy, the Founder of this denomination and Discoverer of Christian Science, as they term her work in affirming the present application of the principles asserted by Jesus, is a most interesting personality. At the risk of colloquialism, I am tempted to "begin at the beginning" of my own knowledge of Mrs. Eddy, and take, as the point of departure, my first meeting with her and the subsequent development of some degree of familiarity with the work of her life which that meeting inaugurated for me.

MRS. EDDY

It was during some year in the early '80's that I became aware — from that close contact with public feeling resulting from editorial work in daily journalism — that the Boston atmosphere was largely thrilled and pervaded by a new and increasing interest in the dominance of mind over matter, and that the central figure in all this agitation was Mrs. Eddy. To a note which I wrote her, begging the favor of an interview for press use, she most kindly replied, naming an evening on which she would receive me. At the hour named I rang the bell at a spacious house on Columbus Avenue, and I was hardly more than seated before Mrs. Eddy entered the room. She impressed me as singularly graceful and winning in bearing and manner, and with great claim to personal beauty. Her figure was tall, slender, and as flexible in movement as that of a Del-

sarte disciple; her face, framed in dark hair and lighted
by luminous blue eyes, had the transparency and rose-flush
of tint so often seen in New England, and she was magnetic,
earnest, impassioned. No photographs can do the least
justice to Mrs. Eddy, as her beautiful complexion and
changeful expression cannot thus be reproduced. At once
one would perceive that she had the temperament to domi-
nate, to lead, to control, not by any crude self-assertion, but
a spiritual animus. Of course such a personality, with the
wonderful tumult in the air that her large and enthusiastic
following excited, fascinated the imagination. What had
she originated? I mentally questioned this modern St.
Catherine, who was dominating her followers like any ab-
bess of old. She told me the story of her life, so far as outward events may translate those inner experiences which
alone are significant.

Mary Baker was the daughter of Mark and Abigail
(Ambrose) Baker, and was born in Concord, N. H., some-
where in the early decade of 1820–'30. At the time I met
her she must have been some sixty years of age, yet she had
the coloring and the elastic bearing of a woman of thirty,
and this, she told me, was due to the principles of Christian Science. On her father's side Mrs. Eddy came from
Scotch and English ancestry, and Hannah More was a
relative of her grandmother. Deacon Ambrose, her mater-
nal grandfather, was known as a "godly man," and her
mother was a religious enthusiast, a saintly and consecrated
character. One of her brothers, Albert Baker, graduated
at Dartmouth and achieved eminence as a lawyer.

MRS. EDDY AS A CHILD

As a child Mary Baker saw visions and dreamed dreams. When eight years of age she began, like Jeanne d'Arc, to hear "voices," and for a year she heard her name called distinctly, and would often run to her mother questioning if she were wanted. One night the mother related to her the story of Samuel, and bade her, if she heard the voice again to reply as he did: "Speak, Lord, for Thy servant heareth." The call came, but the little maid was afraid and did not reply. This caused her tears of remorse and she prayed for forgiveness, and promised to reply if the call came again. It came, and she answered as her mother had bidden her, and after that it ceased.

These experiences, of which Catholic biographies are full, and which history not infrequently emphasizes, certainly offer food for meditation. Theodore Parker related that when he was a lad, at work in a field one day on his father's farm at Lexington, an old man with a snowy beard suddenly appeared at his side, and walked with him as he worked, giving him high counsel and serious thought. All inquiry in the neighborhood as to whence the stranger came or whither he went was fruitless; no one else had seen him, and Mr. Parker always believed, so a friend has told me, that his visitor was a spiritual form from another world. It is certainly true that many and many persons, whose life has been destined to more than ordinary achievement, have had experiences of voices or visions in their early youth.

At an early age Miss Baker was married to Colonel Glover, of Charleston, S. C., who lived only a year. She returned to her father's home — in 1844 — and from that time until 1866 no special record is to be made.

In 1866, while living in Lynn, Mass., Mrs. Eddy (then Mrs. Glover) met with a severe accident, and her case was pronounced hopeless by the physicians. There came a Sunday morning when her pastor came to bid her good-by before proceeding to his morning service, as there was no probability that she would be alive at its close. During this time she suddenly became aware of a divine illumination and ministration. She requested those with her to withdraw, and reluctantly they did so, believing her delirious. Soon, to their bewilderment and fright, she walked into the adjoining room, "and they thought I had died, and that it was my apparition," she said.

THE PRINCIPLE OF DIVINE HEALING

From that hour dated her conviction of the Principle of divine healing, and that it is as true to-day as it was in the days when Jesus of Nazareth walked the earth. "I felt that the divine Spirit had wrought a miracle," she said, in reference to this experience. "How, I could not tell, but later I found it to be in perfect scientific accord with the divine law." From 1866–'69 Mrs. Eddy withdrew from the world to meditate, to pray, to search the Scriptures.

"During this time," she said, in reply to my questions, "the Bible was my only textbook. It answered my questions as to the process by which I was restored to health;

it came to me with a new meaning, and suddenly I appre- 1
hended the spiritual meaning of the teaching of Jesus and
the Principle and the law involved in spiritual Science 3
and metaphysical healing — in a word — Christian
Science."

Mrs. Eddy came to perceive that Christ's healing was not 6
miraculous, but was simply a natural fulfilment of divine
law — a law as operative in the world to-day as it was
nineteen hundred years ago. "Divine Science is begotten 9
of spirituality," she says, "since only the 'pure in heart'
can see God."

In writing of this experience, Mrs. Eddy has said: — 12
"I had learned that thought must be spiritualized in
order to apprehend Spirit. It must become honest, unselfish, and pure, in order to have the least understanding 15
of God in divine Science. The first must become last.
Our reliance upon material things must be transferred to
a perception of and dependence on spiritual things. For 18
Spirit to be supreme in demonstration, it must be supreme
in our affections, and we must be clad with divine power.
I had learned that Mind reconstructed the body, and that 21
nothing else could. All Science is a revelation."

Through homœopathy, too, Mrs. Eddy became convinced of the Principle of Mind-healing, discovering that 24
the more attenuated the drug, the more potent was its
effects.

In 1877 Mrs. Glover married Dr. Asa Gilbert Eddy, of 27
Londonderry, Vermont, a physician who had come into
sympathy with her own views, and who was the first to
place "Christian Scientist" on the sign at his door. Dr. 30

1 Eddy died in 1882, a year after her founding of the Metaphysical College in Boston, in which he taught.

3   The work in the Metaphysical College lasted nine years,
and it was closed (in 1889) in the very zenith of its prosperity, as Mrs. Eddy felt it essential to the deeper founda-
6 tion of her religious work to retire from active contact with
the world.   To this College came hundreds and hundreds
of students, from Europe as well as this country.   I was
9 present at the class lectures now and then, by Mrs. Eddy's
kind invitation, and such earnestness of attention as was
given to her morning talks by the men and women present
12 I never saw equalled.

MRS. EDDY'S PERSONALITY

   On the evening that I first met Mrs. Eddy by her hos-
15 pitable courtesy, I went to her peculiarly fatigued.   I came
away in a state of exhilaration and energy that made me
feel I could have walked any conceivable distance.   I have
18 met Mrs. Eddy many times since then, and always with
this experience repeated.

   Several years ago Mrs. Eddy removed from Columbus
21 to Commonwealth Avenue, where, just beyond Massachusetts Avenue, at the entrance to the Back Bay Park,
she bought one of the most beautiful residences in Boston.
24 The interior is one of the utmost taste and luxury, and the
house is now occupied by Judge and Mrs. Hanna, who are
the editors of *The Christian Science Journal,* a monthly
27 publication, and to whose courtesy I am much indebted
for some of the data of this paper.   "It is a pleasure to

give any information for *The Inter-Ocean*," remarked
Mrs. Hanna, "for it is the great daily that is so fair and so
just in its attitude toward all questions."

The increasing demands of the public on Mrs. Eddy
have been, it may be, one factor in her removal to Concord,
N. H., where she has a beautiful residence, called Pleasant
View. Her health is excellent, and although her hair is
white, she retains in a great degree her energy and power;
she takes a daily walk and drives in the afternoon. She
personally attends to a vast correspondence; superin-
tends the church in Boston, and is engaged on further
writings on Christian Science. In every sense she is the
recognized head of the Christian Science Church. At the
same time it is her most earnest aim to eliminate the element of personality from the faith. "On this point, Mrs.
Eddy feels very strongly," said a gentleman to me on
Christmas eve, as I sat in the beautiful drawing-room,
where Judge and Mrs. Hanna, Miss Elsie Lincoln, the
soprano for the choir of the new church, and one or two
other friends were gathered.

"Mother feels very strongly," he continued, "the danger
and the misfortune of a church depending on any one
personality. It is difficult not to centre too closely around
a highly gifted personality."

THE FIRST ASSOCIATION

The first Christian Scientist Association was organized
on July 4, 1876, by seven persons, including Mrs. Eddy.
In April, 1879, the church was founded with twenty-six

members, and its charter obtained the following June.*
Mrs. Eddy had preached in other parishes for five years
before being ordained in this church, which ceremony
took place in 1881.

The first edition of Mrs. Eddy's book, Science and
Health, was issued in 1875. During these succeeding
twenty years it has been greatly revised and enlarged, and
it is now in its ninety-first edition. It consists of fourteen
chapters, whose titles are as follows: "Science, Theology,
Medicine," "Physiology," "Footsteps of Truth," "Crea-
tion," "Science of Being," "Christian Science and Spiritualism," "Marriage," "Animal Magnetism," "Some
Objections Answered," "Prayer," "Atonement and Eu-
charist," "Christian Science Practice," "Teaching Christian Science," "Recapitulation." Key to the Scriptures,
Genesis, Apocalypse, and Glossary.

The Christian Scientists do not accept the belief we call
spiritualism. They believe those who have passed the
change of death are in so entirely different a plane of consciousness that between the embodied and disembodied
there is no possibility of communication.

They are diametrically opposed to the philosophy of
Karma and of reincarnation, which are the tenets of
theosophy. They hold with strict fidelity to what they
believe to be the literal teachings of Christ.

Yet each and all these movements, however they may
differ among themselves, are phases of idealism and manifestations of a higher spirituality seeking expression.

It is good that each and all shall prosper, serving those
who find in one form of belief or another their best aid

* Steps were taken to promote the Church of Christ, Scientist, in April, May
and June; formal organization was accomplished and the charter obtained in
August, 1879.

and guidance, and that all meet on common ground in the   1
great essentials of love to God and love to man as a signal
proof of the divine origin of humanity which finds no rest   3
until it finds the peace of the Lord in spirituality.   They
all teach that one great truth, that

> God's greatness flows around our incompleteness,   6
> Round our restlessness, His rest.
> ELIZABETH BARRETT BROWNING.

I add on the following page a little poem that I con-   9
sider superbly sweet — from my friend, Miss Whiting,
the talented author of "The World Beautiful." — M. B.
EDDY.   12

AT THE WINDOW

[Written for the *Traveller*]

The sunset, burning low,   15
  Throws o'er the Charles its flood of golden light.
Dimly, as in a dream, I watch the flow
  Of waves of light.   18

The splendor of the sky
  Repeats its glory in the river's flow;
And sculptured angels, on the gray church tower,   21
  Gaze on the world below.

Dimly, as in a dream,
  I see the hurrying throng before me pass,   24
But 'mid them all I only see *one* face,
  Under the meadow grass.

Ah, love! I only know
   How thoughts of you forever cling to me:
I wonder how the seasons come and go
   Beyond the sapphire sea?

LILIAN WHITING.

April 15, 1888.

———

[*Boston Herald*, January 7, 1895]

[Extract]

A TEMPLE GIVEN TO GOD — DEDICATION OF THE MOTHER CHURCH OF CHRISTIAN SCIENCE

NOVEL METHOD OF ENABLING SIX THOUSAND BELIEVERS TO ATTEND THE EXERCISES — THE SERVICE REPEATED FOUR TIMES — SERMON BY REV. MARY BAKER EDDY, FOUNDER OF THE DENOMINATION — BEAUTIFUL ROOM WHICH THE CHILDREN BUILT

With simple ceremonies, four times repeated, in the presence of four different congregations, aggregating nearly six thousand persons, the unique and costly edifice erected in Boston at Norway and Falmouth Streets as a home for The First Church of Christ, Scientist, and a testimonial to the Discoverer and Founder of Christian Science, Rev. Mary Baker Eddy, was yesterday dedicated to the worship of God.

The structure came forth from the hands of the artisans
with every stone paid for — with an appeal, not for more
money, but for a cessation of the tide of contributions
which continued to flow in after the full amount needed
was received. From every State in the Union, and from
many lands, the love-offerings of the disciples of Christian
Science came to help erect this beautiful structure, and
more than four thousand of these contributors came to
Boston, from the far-off Pacific coast and the Gulf States
and all the territory that lies between, to view the new-
built temple and to listen to the Message sent them by
the teacher they revere.

From all New England the members of the denomination gathered; New York sent its hundreds, and even
from the distant States came parties of forty and fifty.
The large auditorium, with its capacity for holding from
fourteen hundred to fifteen hundred persons, was hopelessly
incapable of receiving this vast throng, to say nothing of
nearly a thousand local believers. Hence the service was
repeated until all who wished had heard and seen; and
each of the four vast congregations filled the church to
repletion.

At 7:30 a. m. the chimes in the great stone tower, which
rises one hundred and twenty-six feet above the earth,
rung out their message of "On earth peace, good will
toward men."

Old familiar hymns — "All hail the power of Jesus'
name," and others such — were chimed until the hour for
the dedication service had come.

At 9 a. m. the first congregation gathered. Before this

1 service had closed the large vestry room and the spacious
lobbies and the sidewalks around the church were all
3 filled with a waiting multitude. At 10:30 o'clock another
service began, and at noon still another. Then there was
an intermission, and at 3 p. m. the service was repeated
6 for the last time.

There was scarcely even a minor variation in the exercises at any one of these services. At 10:30 a. m., how-
9 ever, the scene was rendered particularly interesting by
the presence of several hundred children in the central
pews. These were the little contributors to the building
12 fund, whose money was devoted to the "Mother's Room,"
a superb apartment intended for the sole use of Mrs. Eddy.
These children are known in the church as the "Busy
15 Bees," and each of them wore a white satin badge with a
golden beehive stamped upon it, and beneath the beehive
the words, "Mother's Room," in gilt letters.

18 The pulpit end of the auditorium was rich with the
adornment of flowers. On the wall of the choir gallery
above the platform, where the organ is to be hereafter
21 placed, a huge seven-pointed star was hung — a star of
lilies resting on palms, with a centre of white immortelles,
upon which in letters of red were the words: "Love-
24 Children's Offering — 1894."

In the choir and the steps of the platform were potted
palms and ferns and Easter lilies. The desk was wreathed
27 with ferns and pure white roses fastened with a broad
ribbon bow. On its right was a large basket of white
carnations resting on a mat of palms, and on its left a vase
30 filled with beautiful pink roses.

Two combined choirs — that of First Church of Christ, Scientist, of New York, and the choir of the home church, numbering thirty-five singers in all — led the singing, under the direction, respectively, of Mr. Henry Lincoln Case and Miss Elsie Lincoln.

Judge S. J. Hanna, editor of *The Christian Science Journal*, presided over the exercises. On the platform with him were Messrs. Ira O. Knapp, Joseph Armstrong, Stephen A. Chase, and William B. Johnson, who compose the Board of Directors, and Mrs. Henrietta Clark Bemis, a distinguished elocutionist, and a native of Concord, New Hampshire.

The utmost simplicity marked the exercises. After an organ voluntary, the hymn, *"Laus Deo, it is done!"* written by Mrs. Eddy for the corner-stone laying last spring, was sung by the congregation. Selections from the Scriptures and from "Science and Health with Key to the Scriptures," were read by Judge Hanna and Dr. Eddy.

A few minutes of silent prayer came next, followed by the recitation of the Lord's Prayer, with its spiritual interpretation as given in the Christian Science textbook.

The sermon prepared for the occasion by Mrs. Eddy, which was looked forward to as the chief feature of the dedication, was then read by Mrs. Bemis. Mrs. Eddy remained at her home in Concord, N. H., during the day, because, as heretofore stated in *The Herald*, it is her custom to discourage among her followers that sort of personal worship which religious teachers so often receive.

Before presenting the sermon, Mrs. Bemis read the following letter from a former pastor of the church: —

"To Rev. Mary Baker Eddy.

"Dear Teacher, Leader, Guide: — '*Laus Deo,* it is done!'

At last you begin to see the fruition of that you have worked, toiled, prayed for. The 'prayer in stone' is accomplished. Across two thousand miles of space, as mortal sense puts it, I send my hearty congratulations. You are fully occupied, but I thought you would willingly pause for an instant to receive this brief message of congratulation. Surely it marks an era in the blessed onward work of Christian Science. It is a most auspicious hour in your eventful career. While we all rejoice, yet the mother in Israel, alone of us all, comprehends its full significance.

"Yours lovingly,

"LANSON P. NORCROSS."

———

[*Boston Sunday Globe,* January 6, 1895]

[Extract]

STATELY HOME FOR BELIEVERS IN GOSPEL HEALING — A WOMAN OF WEALTH WHO DEVOTES ALL TO HER CHURCH WORK

Christian Science has shown its power over its students, as they are called, by building a church by voluntary contributions, the first of its kind; a church which will be dedicated to-day with a quarter of a million dollars expended and free of debt.

The money has flowed in from all parts of the United States and Canada without any special appeal, and it kept coming until the custodian of funds cried "enough" and refused to accept any further checks by mail or otherwise.

Men, women, and children lent a helping hand, some giving a mite and some substantial sums. Sacrifices were made in many an instance which will never be known in this world.

Christian Scientists not only say that they can effect cures of disease and erect churches, but add that they can get their buildings finished on time, even when the feat seems impossible to mortal senses. Read the following, from a publication of the new denomination: —

"One of the grandest and most helpful features of this glorious consummation is this: that one month before the close of the year every evidence of material sense declared that the church's completion within the year 1894 transcended human possibility. The predictions of workman and onlooker alike were that it could not be completed before April or May of 1895. Much was the ridicule heaped upon the hopeful, trustful ones, who declared and repeatedly asseverated to the contrary. This is indeed, then, a scientific demonstration. It has proved, in most striking manner, the oft-repeated declarations of our textbooks, that the evidence of the mortal senses is unreliable."

A week ago Judge Hanna withdrew from the pastorate of the church, saying he gladly laid down his responsibilities to be succeeded by the grandest of ministers — the Bible and "Science and Health with Key to the Scriptures." This action, it appears, was the result of rules made by Mrs. Eddy. The sermons hereafter will consist of passages read from the two books by Readers, who will be elected each year by the congregation.

1   A story has been abroad that Judge Hanna was so elo-
quent and magnetic that he was attracting listeners who
3 came to hear him preach, rather than in search of the
truth as taught. Consequently the new rules were formu-
lated. But at Christian Science headquarters this is denied;
6 Mrs. Eddy says the words of the judge speak to the point,
and that no such inference is to be drawn therefrom.

In Mrs. Eddy's personal reminiscences, which are pub-
9 lished under the title of "Retrospection and Introspection,"
much is told of herself in detail that can only be touched
upon in this brief sketch.

12 Aristocratic to the backbone, Mrs. Eddy takes delight
in going back to the ancestral tree and in tracing those
branches which are identified with good and great names
15 both in Scotland and England.

Her family came to this country not long before the
Revolution. Among the many souvenirs that Mrs. Eddy
18 remembers as belonging to her grandparents was a heavy
sword, encased in a brass scabbard, upon which had been
inscribed the name of the kinsman upon whom the sword
21 had been bestowed by Sir William Wallace of mighty
Scottish fame.

Mrs. Eddy applied herself, like other girls, to her studies,
24 though perhaps with an unusual zest, delighting in philosophy, logic, and moral science, as well as looking into the
ancient languages, Hebrew, Greek, and Latin.

27 Her last marriage was in the spring of 1877, when, at
Lynn, Mass., she became the wife of Asa Gilbert Eddy.
He was the first organizer of a Christian Science Sunday
30 School, of which he was the superintendent, and later he

attracted the attention of many clergymen of other de- 1
nominations by his able lectures upon Scriptural topics.
He died in 1882. 3

Mrs. Eddy is known to her circle of pupils and admirers
as the editor and publisher of the first official organ of this
sect. It was called the *Journal of Christian Science*, and 6
has had great circulation with the members of this fast-
increasing faith.

In recounting her experiences as the pioneer of Chris- 9
tian Science, she states that she sought knowledge concerning the physical side in this research through the different
schools of allopathy, homœopathy, and so forth, without 12
receiving any real satisfaction. No ancient or modern
philosophy gave her any distinct statement of the Science
of Mind-healing. She claims that no human reason has 15
been equal to the question. And she also defines carefully the difference in the theories between faith-cure and
Christian Science, dwelling particularly upon the terms 18
belief and understanding, which are the key words respectively used in the definitions of these two healing arts.

Besides her Boston home, Mrs. Eddy has a delightful 21
country home one mile from the State House of New
Hampshire's quiet capital, an easy driving distance for
her when she wishes to catch a glimpse of the world. But 24
for the most part she lives very much retired, driving rather
into the country, which is so picturesque all about Concord and its surrounding villages. 27

The big house, so delightfully remodelled and modern-
ized from a primitive homestead that nothing is left ex-
cepting the angles and pitch of the roof, is remarkably 30

well placed upon a terrace that slopes behind the buildings, while they themselves are in the midst of green
stretches of lawns, dotted with beds of flowering shrubs,
with here and there a fountain or summer-house.

Mrs. Eddy took the writer straight to her beloved "look-
out" — a broad piazza on the south side of the second
story of the house, where she can sit in her swinging chair,
revelling in the lights and shades of spring and summer
greenness. Or, as just then, in the gorgeous October
coloring of the whole landscape that lies below, across the
farm, which stretches on through an intervale of beautiful
meadows and pastures to the woods that skirt the valley
of the little truant river, as it wanders eastward.

It pleased her to point out her own birthplace. Straight
as the crow flies, from her piazza, does it lie on the brow
of Bow hill, and then she paused and reminded the reporter
that Congressman Baker from New Hampshire, her cousin,
was born and bred in that same neighborhood. The
photograph of Hon. Hoke Smith, another distinguished
relative, adorned the mantel.

Then my eye caught her family coat of arms and the
diploma given her by the Society of the Daughters of the
Revolution.

The natural and lawful pride that comes with a tincture
of blue and brave blood, is perhaps one of her characteris-
tics, as is many another well-born woman's. She had a
long list of worthy ancestors in Colonial and Revolutionary
days, and the McNeils and General Knox figure largely in
her genealogy, as well as the hero who killed the ill-starred
Paugus.

This big, sunny room which Mrs. Eddy calls her den — or sometimes "Mother's room," when speaking of her many followers who consider her their spiritual Leader — has the air of hospitality that marks its hostess herself. Mrs. Eddy has hung its walls with reproductions of some of Europe's masterpieces, a few of which had been the gifts of her loving pupils.

Looking down from the windows upon the tree-tops on the lower terrace, the reporter exclaimed: "You have lived here only four years, and yet from a barren waste of most unpromising ground has come forth all this beauty!"

"Four years!" she ejaculated; "two and a half, only two and a half years." Then, touching my sleeve and pointing, she continued: "Look at those big elms! I had them brought here in warm weather, almost as big as they are now, and not one died."

Mrs. Eddy talked earnestly of her friendships. . . . She told something of her domestic arrangements, of how she had long wished to get away from her busy career in Boston, and return to her native granite hills, there to build a substantial home that should do honor to that precinct of Concord.

She chose the stubbly old farm on the road from Concord, within one mile of the "Eton of America," St. Paul's School. Once bought, the will of the woman set at work, and to-day a strikingly well-kept estate is the first impression given to the visitor as he approaches Pleasant View.

She employs a number of men to keep the grounds and farm in perfect order, and it was pleasing to learn that this

1 rich woman is using her money to promote the welfare of
industrious workmen, in whom she takes a vital interest.

3   Mrs. Eddy believes that "the laborer is worthy of his
hire," and, moreover, that he deserves to have a home and
family of his own. Indeed, one of her motives in buying
6 so large an estate was that she might do something for the
toilers, and thus add her influence toward the advancement
of better home life and citizenship.

9   [*Boston Transcript*, December 31, 1894]
                    [Extract]

The growth of Christian Science is properly marked by
12 the erection of a visible house of worship in this city, which
will be dedicated to-morrow. It has cost two hundred
thousand dollars, and no additional sums outside of the
15 subscriptions are asked for. This particular phase of
religious belief has impressed itself upon a large and increasing number of Christian people, who have been
18 tempted to examine its principles, and doubtless have been
comforted and strengthened by them. Any new movement will awaken some sort of interest. There are many
21 who have worn off the novelty and are thoroughly carried
away with the requirements, simple and direct as they are,
of Christian Science. The opposition against it from the
24 so-called orthodox religious bodies keeps up a while, but
after a little skirmishing, finally subsides. No one religious
body holds the whole of truth, and whatever is likely to
27 show even some one side of it will gain followers and live
down any attempted repression.

Christian Science does not strike all as a system of truth. If it did, it would be a prodigy. Neither does the Christian faith produce the same impressions upon all. Freedom to believe or to dissent is a great privilege in these days. So when a number of conscientious followers apply themselves to a matter like Christian Science, they are enjoying that liberty which is their inherent right as human beings, and though they cannot escape censure, yet they are to be numbered among the many pioneers who are searching after religious truth. There is really nothing settled. Every truth is more or less in a state of agitation. The many who have worked in the mine of knowledge are glad to welcome others who have different methods, and with them bring different ideas.

It is too early to predict where this movement will go, and how greatly it will affect the well-established methods. That it has produced a sensation in religious circles, and called forth the implements of theological warfare, is very well known. While it has done this, it may, on the other hand, have brought a benefit. Ere this many a new project in religious belief has stirred up feeling, but as time has gone on, compromises have been welcomed.

The erection of this temple will doubtless help on the growth of its principles. Pilgrims from everywhere will go there in search of truth, and some may be satisfied and some will not. Christian Science cannot absorb the world's thought. It may get the share of attention it deserves, but it can only aspire to take its place alongside other great demonstrations of religious belief which have done something good for the sake of humanity.

Wonders will never cease. Here is a church whose treasurer has to send out word that no sums except those already subscribed can be received! The Christian Scientists have a faith of the mustard-seed variety. What a pity some of our practical Christian folk have not a faith approximate to that of these "impractical" Christian Scientists.

[*Jackson Patriot*, Jackson, Mich., January 20, 1895]

[Extract]

CHRISTIAN SCIENCE

The erection of a massive temple in Boston by Christian Scientists, at a cost of over two hundred thousand dollars, love-offerings of the disciples of Mary Baker Eddy, reviver of the ancient faith and author of the textbook from which, with the New Testament at the foundation, believers receive light, health, and strength, is evidence of the rapid growth of the new movement. We call it new. It is not. The name Christian Science alone is new. At the beginning of Christianity it was taught and practised by Jesus and his disciples. The Master was the great healer. But the wave of materialism and bigotry that swept over the world for fifteen centuries, covering it with the blackness of the Dark Ages, nearly obliterated all vital belief in his teachings. The Bible was a sealed book. Recently a revived belief in what he taught is manifest, and Christian Science is one result. No new doctrine is proclaimed, but

there is the fresh development of a Principle that was put
into practice by the Founder of Christianity nineteen hundred years ago, though practised in other countries at an
earlier date. "The thing that hath been, it is that which
shall be; and that which is done is that which shall be
done: and there is no new thing under the sun."

The condition which Jesus of Nazareth, on various
occasions during the three years of his ministry on earth,
declared to be essential, in the mind of both healer and
patient, is contained in the one word — *faith*. Can drugs
suddenly cure leprosy? When the ten lepers were cleansed
and one returned to give thanks in Oriental phrase, Jesus
said to him: "Arise, go thy way: thy faith hath made thee
whole." That was Christian Science. In his "Law of
Psychic Phenomena" Hudson says: "That word, more
than any other, expresses the whole law of human felicity
and power in this world, and of salvation in the world to
come. It is that attribute of mind which elevates man
above the level of the brute, and gives dominion over the
physical world. It is the essential element of success in
every field of human endeavor. It constitutes the power
of the human soul. When Jesus of Nazareth proclaimed
its potency from the hilltops of Palestine, he gave to mankind the key to health and heaven, and earned the title
of Saviour of the World." Whittier, grandest of mystic
poets, saw the truth: —

> That healing gift he lends to them
>   Who use it in his name;
> The power that filled his garment's hem
>   Is evermore the same.

Again, in a poem entitled "The Master," he wrote: —

> The healing of his seamless dress
>   Is by our beds of pain;
> We touch him in life's throng and press,
>   And we are whole again.[1]

That Jesus operated in perfect harmony with natural law, not in defiance, suppression, or violation of it, we cannot doubt. The perfectly natural is the perfectly spiritual. Jesus enunciated and exemplified the Principle; and, obviously, the conditions requisite in psychic healing to-day are the same as were necessary in apostolic times. We accept the statement of Hudson: "There was no law of nature violated or transcended. On the contrary, the whole transaction was in perfect obedience to the laws of nature. He understood the law perfectly, as no one before him understood it; and in the plenitude of his power he applied it where the greatest good could be accomplished." A careful reading of the accounts of his healings, in the light of modern science, shows that he observed, in his practice of mental therapeutics, the conditions of environment and harmonious influence that are essential to success. In the case of Jairus' daughter they are fully set forth. He kept the unbelievers away, "put them all out," and permitting only the father and mother, with his closest friends and followers, Peter, James, and John, in the chamber with him, and having thus the most perfect obtainable environment, he raised the daughter to life.

[1] NOTE: — About 1868, the author of Science and Health healed Mr. Whittier with one visit, at his home in Amesbury, of incipient pulmonary consumption. — M. B. EDDY.

> "Not in blind caprice of will,   1
> Not in cunning sleight of skill,
> Not for show of power, was wrought   3
> Nature's marvel in thy thought."

In a previous article we have referred to cyclic changes
that came during the last quarter of preceding centuries. 6
Of our remarkable nineteenth century not the least eventful circumstance is the advent of Christian Science.
That it should be the work of a woman is the natural out- 9
come of a period notable for her emancipation from many
of the thraldoms, prejudices, and oppressions of the past.
We do not, therefore, regard it as a mere coincidence that 12
the first edition of Mrs. Eddy's Science and Health should
have been published in 1875. Since then she has revised
it many times, and the ninety-first edition is announced. 15
Her discovery was first called, "The Science of Divine
Metaphysical Healing." Afterward she selected the name
Christian Science. It is based upon what is held to be 18
scientific certainty, namely, — that all causation is of
Mind, every effect has its origin in desire and thought.
The theology — if we may use the word — of Christian 21
Science is contained in the volume entitled "Science and
Health with Key to the Scriptures."

The present Boston congregation was organized 24
April 19, 1879, and has now over four thousand members.
It is regarded as the parent organization, all others being
branches, though each is entirely independent in the 27
management of its own affairs. Truth is the sole recognized
authority. Of actual members of different congregations
there are between one hundred thousand and two hundred 30

thousand. One or more organized societies have sprung
up in New York, Chicago, Buffalo, Cleveland, Cincin-
nati, Philadelphia, Detroit, Toledo, Milwaukee, Madison,
Scranton, Peoria, Atlanta, Toronto, and nearly every other
centre of population, besides a large and growing number
of receivers of the faith among the members of all the
churches and non-church-going people. In some churches
a majority of the members are Christian Scientists, and, as
a rule, are the most intelligent.

Space does not admit of an elaborate presentation on the
occasion of the erection of the temple, in Boston, the
dedication taking place on the 6th of January, of one of
the most remarkable, helpful, and powerful movements
of the last quarter of the century. Christian Science
has brought hope and comfort to many weary souls. It
makes people better and happier. Welding Christianity
and Science, hitherto divorced because dogma and truth
could not unite, was a happy inspiration.

> "And still we love the evil cause,
>   And of the just effect complain;
> We tread upon life's broken laws,
>   And mourn our self-inflicted pain."

[*The Outlook*, New York, January 19, 1895]

A CHRISTIAN SCIENCE CHURCH

A great Christian Science church was dedicated in Boston on Sunday, the 6th inst. It is located at Norway and
Falmouth Streets, and is intended to be a testimonial to

the Discoverer and Founder of Christian Science, the
Rev. Mary Baker Eddy. The building is fire-proof, and
cost over two hundred thousand dollars. It is entirely
paid for, and contributions for its erection came from every
State in the Union, and from many lands. The auditorium
is said to seat between fourteen and fifteen hundred, and
was thronged at the four services on the day of dedication.
The sermon, prepared by Mrs. Eddy, was read by Mrs.
Bemis. It rehearsed the significance of the building, and
reenunciated the truths which will find emphasis there.
From the description we judge that it is one of the most
beautiful buildings in Boston, and, indeed, in all New
England. Whatever may be thought of the peculiar tenets
of the Christian Scientists, and whatever difference of
opinion there may be concerning the organization of such
a church, there can be no question but that the adherents
of this church have proved their faith by their works.

[*American Art Journal*, New York, January 26, 1895]

"Our Prayer in Stone"

Such is the excellent name given to a new Boston church.
Few people outside its own circles realize how extensive is
the belief in Christian Science. There are several sects of
mental healers, but this new edifice on Back Bay, just off
Huntington Avenue, not far from the big Mechanics
Building and the proposed site of the new Music Hall,
belongs to the followers of Rev. Mary Baker Glover Eddy,
a lady born of an old New Hampshire family, who, after

1 many vicissitudes, found herself in Lynn, Mass., healed by
the power of divine Mind, and thereupon devoted herself
3 to imparting this faith to her fellow-beings. Coming to
Boston about 1880, she began teaching, gathered an
association of students, and organized a church. For
6 several years past she has lived in Concord, N. H., near
her birthplace, owning a beautiful estate called Pleasant
View; but thousands of believers throughout this country
9 have joined The Mother Church in Boston, and have now
erected this edifice at a cost of over two hundred thousand
dollars, every bill being paid.

12 Its appearance is shown in the pictures we are permitted
to publish. In the belfry is a set of tubular chimes. Inside
is a basement room, capable of division into seven excellent
15 class-rooms, by the use of movable partitions. The main
auditorium has wide galleries, and will seat over a thousand
in its exceedingly comfortable pews. Scarcely any wood-
18 work is to be found. The floors are all mosaic, the steps
marble, and the walls stone. It is rather dark, often too
much so for comfortable reading, as all the windows are of
21 colored glass, with pictures symbolic of the tenets of the
organization. In the ceiling is a beautiful sunburst window.
Adjoining the chancel is a pastor's study; but for an
24 indefinite time their prime instructor has ordained that the
only pastor shall be the Bible, with her book, called
"Science and Health with Key to the Scriptures." In the
27 tower is a room devoted to her, and called "Mother's
Room," furnished with all conveniences for living, should
she wish to make it a home by day or night. Therein is
30 a portrait of her in stained glass; and an electric light,

behind an antique lamp, kept perpetually burning[1] in her
honor; though she has not yet visited her temple, which
was dedicated on New Year's Sunday in a somewhat novel
way.

There was no special sentence or prayer of consecration,
but continuous services were held from nine to four o'clock,
every hour and a half, so long as there were attendants;
and some people heard these exercises four times repeated.
The printed program was for some reason not followed,
certain hymns and psalms being omitted. There was singing by a choir and congregation. The *Pater Noster* was
repeated in the way peculiar to Christian Scientists, the
congregation repeating one sentence and the leader re-
sponding with its parallel interpretation by Mrs. Eddy.
Antiphonal paragraphs were read from the book of
Revelation and her work respectively. The sermon,
prepared by Mrs. Eddy, was well adapted for its purpose,
and read by a professional elocutionist, not an adherent of
the order, Mrs. Henrietta Clark Bemis, in a clear emphatic
style. The solo singer, however, was a Scientist, Miss Elsie
Lincoln; and on the platform sat Joseph Armstrong,
formerly of Kansas, and now the business manager of the
Publishing Society, with the other members of the Christian
Science Board of Directors — Ira O. Knapp, Edward P.
Bates, Stephen A. Chase, — gentlemen officially connected
with the movement. The children of believing families
collected the money for the Mother's Room, and seats were
especially set apart for them at the second dedicatory
service. Before one service was over and the auditors left
by the rear doors, the front vestibule and street (despite

[1] At Mrs. Eddy's request the lamp was not kept burning.

1 the snowstorm) were crowded with others, waiting for
admission.

3   On the next Sunday the new order of service went
into operation. There was no address of any sort, no
notices, no explanation of Bible or their textbook. Judge
6 Hanna, who was a Colorado lawyer before coming into
this work, presided, reading in clear, manly, and intelligent tones, the *Quarterly* Bible Lesson, which happened
9 that day to be on Jesus' miracle of loaves and fishes.
Each paragraph he supplemented first with illustrative
Scripture parallels, as set down for him, and then by pas-
12 sages selected for him from Mrs. Eddy's book. The place
was again crowded, many having remained over a week
from among the thousands of adherents who had come
15 to Boston for this auspicious occasion from all parts of
the country. The organ, made by Farrand & Votey in
Detroit, at a cost of eleven thousand dollars, is the gift of
18 a wealthy Universalist gentleman, but was not ready for
the opening. It is to fill the recess behind the spacious
platform, and is described as containing pneumatic wind-
21 chests throughout, and having an Æolian attachment.
It is of three-manual compass, C. C. C. to C. 4, 61 notes;
and pedal compass, C. C. C. to F. 30. The great organ
24 has double open diapason (stopped bass), open diapason,
dulciana, viola di gamba, doppel flute, hohl flute, octave,
octave quint, superoctave, and trumpet, — 61 pipes each.
27 The swell organ has bourdon, open diapason, salicional,
æoline, stopped diapason, gemshorn, flute harmonique,
flageolet, cornet — 3 ranks, 183, — cornopean, oboe, vox
30 humana — 61 pipes each. The choir organ, enclosed in

separate swell-box, has geigen principal, dolce, concert
flute, quintadena, fugara, flute d'amour, piccolo harmonique, clarinet, — 61 pipes each. The pedal organ has
open diapason, bourdon, lieblich gedeckt (from stop 10),
violoncello-wood, — 30 pipes each. Couplers: swell to
great; choir to great; swell to choir; swell to great octaves, swell to great sub-octaves; choir to great sub-
octaves; swell octaves; swell to pedal; great to pedal;
choir to pedal. Mechanical accessories: swell tremulant,
choir tremulant, bellows signal; wind indicator. Pedal
movements: three affecting great and pedal stops, three
affecting swell and pedal stops; great to pedal reversing
pedal; crescendo and full organ pedal; balanced great
and choir pedal; balanced swell pedal.

Beautiful suggestions greet you in every part of this
unique church, which is practical as well as poetic, and
justifies the name given by Mrs. Eddy, which stands at
the head of this sketch. J. H. W.

[*Boston Journal*, January 7, 1895]

CHIMES RANG SWEETLY

Much admiration was expressed by all those fortunate
enough to listen to the first peal of the chimes in the tower
of The First Church of Christ, Scientist, corner of Falmouth and Norway Streets, dedicated yesterday. The
sweet, musical tones attracted quite a throng of people,
who listened with delight.

The chimes were made by the United States Tubular

Bell Company, of Methuen, Mass., and are something of a novelty in this country, though for some time well and favorably known in the Old Country, especially in England.

They are a substitution of tubes of drawn brass for the heavy cast bells of old-fashioned chimes. They have the advantage of great economy of space, as well as of cost, a chime of fifteen bells occupying a space not more than five by eight feet.

Where the old-fashioned chimes required a strong man to ring them, these can be rung from an electric keyboard, and even when rung by hand require but little muscular power to manipulate them and call forth all the purity and sweetness of their tones. The quality of tone is something superb, being rich and mellow. The tubes are carefully tuned, so that the harmony is perfect. They have all the beauties of a great cathedral chime, with infinitely less expense.

There is practically no limit to the uses to which these bells may be put. They can be called into requisition in theatres, concert halls, and public buildings, as they range in all sizes, from those described down to little sets of silver bells that might be placed on a small centre table.

[*The Republic*, Washington, D. C., February 2, 1895]

[Extract]

CHRISTIAN SCIENCE

MARY BAKER EDDY THE "MOTHER" OF THE IDEA — SHE HAS AN IMMENSE FOLLOWING THROUGHOUT THE UNITED STATES, AND A CHURCH COSTING $250,000 WAS RECENTLY BUILT IN HER HONOR AT BOSTON

"My faith has the strength to nourish trees as well as souls," was the remark Rev. Mary Baker Eddy, the "Mother" of Christian Science, made recently as she pointed to a number of large elms that shade her delightful country home in Concord, N. H. "I had them brought here in warm weather, almost as big as they are now, and not one died." This is a remarkable statement, but it is made by a remarkable woman, who has originated a new phase of religious belief, and who numbers over one hundred thousand intelligent people among her devoted followers.

The great hold she has upon this army was demonstrated in a very tangible and material manner recently, when "The First Church of Christ, Scientist," erected at a cost of two hundred and fifty thousand dollars, was dedicated in Boston. This handsome edifice was paid for before it was begun, by the voluntary contributions of Christian Scientists all over the country, and a tablet imbedded in its wall declares that it was built as "a testimonial to our beloved teacher, Rev. Mary Baker Eddy,

Discoverer and Founder of Christian Science, author of
its textbook, 'Science and Health with Key to the Scriptures,' president of the Massachusetts Metaphysical College, and the first pastor of this denomination.''

There is usually considerable difficulty in securing suffi-
cient funds for the building of a new church, but such was
not the experience of Rev. Mary Baker Eddy. Money
came freely from all parts of the United States. Men,
women, and children contributed, some giving a pittance,
others donating large sums. When the necessary amount
was raised, the custodian of the funds was compelled to
refuse further contributions, in order to stop the continued
inflow of money from enthusiastic Christian Scientists.

Mrs. Eddy says she discovered Christian Science in
1866. She studied the Scriptures and the sciences, she
declares, in a search for the great curative Principle. She
investigated allopathy, homœopathy, and electricity, without finding a clew; and modern philosophy gave her no
distinct statement of the Science of Mind-healing. After
careful study she became convinced that the curative
Principle was the Deity.

[*New York Tribune*, February 7, 1895]

[Extract]

Boston has just dedicated the first church of the Christian Scientists, in commemoration of the Founder of that
sect, the Rev. Mary Baker Eddy, drawing together six
thousand people to participate in the ceremonies, showing

that belief in that curious creed is not confined to its
original apostles and promulgators, but that it has pene-
trated what is called the New England mind to an un-
looked-for extent.   In inviting the Eastern churches and
the Anglican fold to unity with Rome, the Holy Father
should not overlook the Boston sect of Christian Scientists,
which is rather small and new, to be sure, but is undoubt-
edly an interesting faith and may have a future before it,
whatever attitude Rome may assume toward it.

[*Journal*, Kansas City, Mo., January 10, 1895]

[Extract]

GROWTH OF A FAITH

Attention is directed to the progress which has been
made by what is called Christian Science by the dedication
at Boston of "The First Church of Christ, Scientist."
It is a most beautiful structure of gray granite, and its
builders call it their "prayer in stone," which suggests
to recollection the story of the cathedral of Amiens, whose
architectural construction and arrangement of statuary
and paintings made it to be called the Bible of that city.
The Frankish church was reared upon the spot where, in
pagan times, one bitter winter day, a Roman soldier parted
his mantle with his sword and gave half of the garment to
a naked beggar; and so was memorialized in art and
stone what was called the divine spirit of giving, whose un-
believing exemplar afterward became a saint.   The Boston
church similarly expresses the faith of those who believe

1 in what they term the divine art of healing, which, to their
minds, exists as much to-day as it did when Christ healed
3 the sick.

The first church organization of this faith was founded
fifteen years ago with a membership of only twenty-six,
6 and since then the number of believers has grown with
remarkable rapidity, until now there are societies in every
part of the country. This growth, it is said, proceeds
9 more from the graveyards than from conversions from
other churches, for most of those who embrace the faith
claim to have been rescued from death miraculously under
12 the injunction to "heal the sick, cleanse the lepers, raise
the dead, cast out demons." They hold with strict fidelity
to what they conceive to be the literal teachings of the
15 Bible as expressed in its poetical and highly figurative
language.

Altogether the belief and service are well suited to
18 satisfy a taste for the mystical which, along many lines, has
shown an uncommon development in this country during
the last decade, and which is largely Oriental in its choice.
21 Such a rapid departure from long respected views as is
marked by the dedication of this church, and others of
kindred meaning, may reasonably excite wonder as to
24 how radical is to be this encroachment upon prevailing
faiths, and whether some of the pre-Christian ideas of
the Asiatics are eventually to supplant those in company
27 with which our civilization has developed.

[*Montreal Daily Herald*, Saturday, February 2, 1895]   1

[Extract]

CHRISTIAN SCIENCE   3

SKETCH OF ITS ORIGIN AND GROWTH — THE MONTREAL BRANCH

"If you would found a new faith, go to Boston," has
been said by a great American writer. This is no idle   6
word, but a fact borne out by circumstances. Boston can
fairly claim to be the hub of the logical universe, and an
accurate census of the religious faiths which are to be   9
found there to-day would probably show a greater number
of them than even Max O'Rell's famous enumeration of
John Bull's creeds.   12

Christian Science, or the Principle of divine healing,
is one of those movements which seek to give expression
to a higher spirituality. Founded twenty-five years ago, 15
it was still practically unknown a decade since, but to-day
it numbers over a quarter of a million of believers, the
majority of whom are in the United States, and is rapidly 18
growing. In Canada, also, there is a large number of
members. Toronto and Montreal have strong churches,
comparatively, while in many towns and villages single 21
believers or little knots of them are to be found.

It was exactly one hundred years from the date of the
Declaration of Independence, when on July 4, 1876, the 24
first Christian Scientist Association was organized by
seven persons, of whom the foremost was Mrs. Eddy.
The church was founded in April, 1879, with twenty-six 27
members, and a charter was obtained two months later.

Mrs. Eddy assumed the pastorship of the church during its early years, and in 1881 was ordained, being now known as the Rev. Mary Baker Eddy.

The Massachusetts Metaphysical College was founded by Mrs. Eddy in 1881, and here she taught the principles of the faith for nine years. Students came to it in hundreds from all parts of the world, and many are now pastors or in practice. The college was closed in 1889, as Mrs. Eddy felt it necessary for the interests of her religious work to retire from active contact with the world. She now lives in a beautiful country residence in her native State.

[*The American*, Baltimore, Md., January 14, 1895]

[Extract]

Mrs. Eddy's Disciples

It is not generally known that a Christian Science congregation was organized in this city about a year ago. It now holds regular services in the parlor of the residence of the pastor, at 1414 Linden Avenue. The dedication in Boston last Sunday of the Christian Science church, called The Mother Church, which cost over two hundred thousand dollars, adds interest to the Baltimore organization. There are many other church edifices in the United States owned by Christian Scientists. Christian Science was founded by Mrs. Mary Baker Eddy. The Baltimore congregation was organized at a meeting held at the present location on February 27, 1894.

Dr. Hammond, the pastor, came to Baltimore about three years ago to organize this movement. Miss Cross came from Syracuse, N. Y., about eighteen months ago. Both were under the instruction of Mrs. Mary Baker Eddy, the Founder of the movement.

Dr. Hammond says he was converted to Christian Science by being cured by Mrs. Eddy of a physical ailment some twelve years ago, after several doctors had pronounced his case incurable. He says they use no medicines, but rely on Mind for cure, believing that disease comes from evil and sick-producing thoughts, and that, if they can so fill the mind with good thoughts as to leave no room there for the bad, they can work a cure. He distinguishes Christian Science from the faith-cure, and added: "This Christian Science really is a return to the ideas of primitive Christianity. It would take a small book to explain fully all about it, but I may say that the fundamental idea is that God is Mind, and we interpret the Scriptures wholly from the spiritual or metaphysical standpoint. We find in this view of the Bible the power fully developed to heal the sick. It is not faith-cure, but it is an acknowledgment of certain Christian and scientific laws, and to work a cure the practitioner must understand these laws aright. The patient may gain a better understanding than the Church has had in the past. All churches have prayed for the cure of disease, but they have not done so in an intelligent manner, understanding and demonstrating the Christ-healing."

1   [*The Reporter*, Lebanon, Ind., January 18, 1895]

[Extract]

3   DISCOVERED CHRISTIAN SCIENCE

REMARKABLE CAREER OF REV. MARY BAKER EDDY, WHO HAS
OVER ONE HUNDRED THOUSAND FOLLOWERS

6   Rev. Mary Baker Eddy, Discoverer and Founder of
Christian Science, author of its textbook, "Science and
Health with Key to the Scriptures," president of the Mas-
9   sachusetts Metaphysical College, and first pastor of the
Christian Science denomination, is without doubt one of
the most remarkable women in America. She has within a
12   few years founded a sect that has over one hundred thousand converts, and very recently saw completed in Boston,
as a testimonial to her labors, a handsome fire-proof church
15   that cost two hundred and fifty thousand dollars and was
paid for by Christian Scientists all over the country.

Mrs. Eddy asserts that in 1866 she became certain that
18   "all causation was Mind, and every effect a mental phenomenon." Taking her text from the Bible, she endeav-
ored in vain to find the great curative Principle—the Deity
21   — in philosophy and schools of medicine, and she con-
cluded that the way of salvation demonstrated by Jesus
was the power of Truth over all error, sin, sickness, and
24   death. Thus originated the divine or spiritual Science of
Mind-healing, which she termed Christian Science. She
has a palatial home in Boston and a country-seat in
27   Concord, N. H. The Christian Science Church has a

membership of four thousand, and eight hundred of the members are Bostonians.

[*N. Y. Commercial Advertiser*, January 9, 1895]

The idea that Christian Science has declined in popularity is not borne out by the voluntary contribution of a quarter of a million dollars for a memorial church for Mrs. Eddy, the inventor of this cure. The money comes from Christian Science believers exclusively.

[*The Post*, Syracuse, New York, February 1, 1895]

Do Not Believe She Was Deified

CHRISTIAN SCIENTISTS OF SYRACUSE SURPRISED AT THE NEWS ABOUT MRS. MARY BAKER EDDY, FOUNDER OF THE FAITH

Christian Scientists in this city, and in fact all over the country, have been startled and greatly discomfited over the announcements in New York papers that Mrs. Mary Baker G. Eddy, the acknowledged Christian Science Leader, has been exalted by various dignitaries of the faith. . . .

It is well known that Mrs. Eddy has resigned herself completely to the study and foundation of the faith to which many thousands throughout the United States are now so entirely devoted. By her followers and cobelievers she is unquestionably looked upon as having a divine mission to

1 fulfil, and as though inspired in her great task by super-
natural power.

3 For the purpose of learning the feeling of Scientists in this
city toward the reported deification of Mrs. Eddy, a *Post*
reporter called upon a few of the leading members of the
6 faith yesterday and had a number of very interesting con-
versations upon the subject.

Mrs. D. W. Copeland of University Avenue was one of
9 the first to be seen. Mrs. Copeland is a very pleasant and
agreeable lady, ready to converse, and evidently very much
absorbed in the work to which she has given so much of
12 her attention. Mrs. Copeland claims to have been healed
a number of years ago by Christian Scientists, after she
had practically been given up by a number of well-known
15 physicians.

"And for the past eleven years," said Mrs. Copeland,
"I have not taken any medicine or drugs of any kind, and
18 yet have been perfectly well."

In regard to Mrs. Eddy, Mrs. Copeland said that she
was the Founder of the faith, but that she had never
21 claimed, nor did she believe that Mrs. Lathrop had, that
Mrs. Eddy had any power other than that which came
from God and through faith in Him and His teachings.

24 "The power of Christ has been dormant in mankind for
ages," added the speaker, "and it was Mrs. Eddy's mission
to revive it. In our labors we take Christ as an example,
27 going about doing good and healing the sick. Christ has
told us to do his work, naming as one great essential that
we have faith in him.

30 "Did you ever hear of Jesus' taking medicine himself, or

giving it to others?" inquired the speaker. "Then why
should we worry ourselves about sickness and disease?
If we become sick, God will care for us, and will send to
us those who have faith, who believe in His unlimited and
divine power. Mrs. Eddy was strictly an ardent follower
after God. She had faith in Him, and she cured herself of
a deathly disease through the mediation of her God. Then
she secluded herself from the world for three years and
studied and meditated over His divine Word. She delved
deep into the Biblical passages, and at the end of the period
came from her seclusion one of the greatest Biblical scholars of the age. Her mission was then the mission of a
Christian, to do good and heal the sick, and this duty she
faithfully performed. She of herself had no power. But
God has fulfilled His promises to her and to the world.
If you have faith, you can move mountains."

Mrs. Henrietta N. Cole is also a very prominent member
of the church. When seen yesterday she emphasized herself as being of the same theory as Mrs. Copeland. Mrs.
Cole has made a careful and searching study in the beliefs
of Scientists, and is perfectly versed in all their beliefs and
doctrines. She stated that man of himself has no power,
but that all comes from God. She placed no credit whatever in the reports from New York that Mrs. Eddy has
been accredited as having been deified. She referred the
reporter to the large volume which Mrs. Eddy had herself
written, and said that no more complete and yet concise
idea of her belief could be obtained than by a perusal of it.

[*New York Herald*, February 6, 1895]

Mrs. Eddy Shocked

[By Telegraph to the *Herald*]

Concord, N. H., February 4, 1895. — The article published in the *Herald* on January 29, regarding a statement made by Mrs. Laura Lathrop, pastor of the Christian Science congregation that meets every Sunday in Hodgson Hall, New York, was shown to Mrs. Mary Baker Eddy, the Christian Science "Discoverer," to-day.

Mrs. Eddy preferred to prepare a written answer to the interrogatory, which she did in this letter, addressed to the editor of the *Herald:* —

"A despatch is given me, calling for an interview to answer for myself, 'Am I the second Christ?'

"Even the question shocks me. What I am is for God to declare in His infinite mercy. As it is, I claim nothing more than what I am, the Discoverer and Founder of Christian Science, and the blessing it has been to mankind which eternity enfolds.

"I think Mrs. Lathrop was not understood. If she said aught with intention to be thus understood, it is not what I have taught her, and not at all as I have heard her talk.

"My books and teachings maintain but one conclusion and statement of the Christ and the deification of mortals.

"Christ is individual, and one with God, in the sense of divine Love and its compound divine ideal.

"There was, is, and never can be but one God, one

Christ, one Jesus of Nazareth. Whoever in any age ex- 1
presses most of the spirit of Truth and Love, the Principle
of God's idea, has most of the spirit of Christ, of that Mind 3
which was in Christ Jesus.

"If Christian Scientists find in my writings, teachings,
and example a greater degree of this spirit than in others, 6
they can justly declare it. But to think or speak of me in
any manner as a Christ, is sacrilegious. Such a statement
would not only be false, but the absolute antipode of Chris- 9
tian Science, and would savor more of heathenism than of
my doctrines.

"MARY BAKER EDDY."   12

––––––––––

[*The Globe*, Toronto, Canada, January 12, 1895]

[Extract]

CHRISTIAN SCIENTISTS   15

DEDICATION TO THE FOUNDER OF THE ORDER OF A BEAUTIFUL
CHURCH AT BOSTON — MANY TORONTO SCIENTISTS PRESENT

The Christian Scientists of Toronto, to the number of 18
thirty, took part in the ceremonies at Boston last Sunday
and for the day or two following, by which the members
of that faith all over North America celebrated the dedica- 21
tion of the church constructed in the great New England
capital as a testimonial to the Discoverer and Founder of
Christian Science, Rev. Mary Baker Eddy.   24

The temple is believed to be the most nearly fire-proof
church structure on the continent, the only combustible

material used in its construction being that used in the doors and pews. A striking feature of the church is a beautiful apartment known as the "Mother's Room," which is approached through a superb archway of Italian marble set in the wall. The furnishing of the "Mother's Room" is described as "particularly beautiful, and blends harmoniously with the pale green and gold decoration of the walls. The floor is of mosaic in elegant designs, and two alcoves are separated from the apartment by rich hangings of deep green plush, which in certain lights has a shimmer of silver. The furniture frames are of white mahogany in special designs, elaborately carved, and the upholstery is in white and gold tapestry. A superb mantel of Mexican onyx with gold decoration adorns the south wall, and before the hearth is a large rug composed entirely of skins of the eider-down duck, brought from the Arctic regions. Pictures and bric-a-brac everywhere suggest the tribute of loving friends. One of the two alcoves is a retiring-room and the other a lavatory in which the plumbing is all heavily plated with gold."

[*Evening Monitor*, Concord, N. H., February 27, 1895]

An Elegant Souvenir

Rev. Mary Baker Eddy Memorialized By a Christian Science Church

Rev. Mary Baker Eddy, Discoverer of Christian Science, has received from the members of The First Church of Christ, Scientist, Boston, an invitation formally to accept

the magnificent new edifice of worship which the church 1
has just erected.

The invitation itself is one of the most chastely elegant 3
memorials ever prepared, and is a scroll of solid gold,
suitably engraved, and encased in a handsome plush
casket with white silk linings. Attached to the scroll is a 6
golden key of the church structure.

The inscription reads thus: —

Dear Mother: —During the year eighteen hundred and 9
ninety-four a church edifice was erected at the intersection
of Falmouth and Norway Streets, in the city of Boston,
by the loving hands of four thousand members. This 12
edifice is built as a testimonial to Truth, as revealed by
divine Love through you to this age. You are hereby
most lovingly invited to visit and formally accept this 15
testimonial on the twentieth day of February, eighteen
hundred and ninety-five, at high noon.

"The First Church of Christ, Scientist, at Boston, Mass. 18
"By Edward P. Bates,
"Caroline S. Bates.

"To the Reverend Mary Baker Eddy, 21
"Boston, January 6th, 1895."

————

[*People and Patriot*, Concord, N. H., February 27, 1895]

MAGNIFICENT TESTIMONIAL 24

Members of The First Church of Christ, Scientist, at
Boston, have forwarded to Mrs. Mary Baker Eddy of

this city, the Founder of Christian Science, a testimonial which is probably one of the most magnificent examples of the goldsmith's art ever wrought in this country. It is in the form of a gold scroll, twenty-six inches long, nine inches wide, and an eighth of an inch thick.

It bears upon its face the following inscription, cut in script letters: —

"*Dear Mother:* — During the year 1894 a church edifice was erected at the intersection of Falmouth and Norway Streets, in the city of Boston, by the loving hands of four thousand members. This edifice is built as a testimonial to Truth, as revealed by divine Love through you to this age. You are hereby most lovingly invited to visit and formally accept this testimonial on the 20th day of February, 1895, at high noon.

"The First Church of Christ, Scientist, at Boston, Mass.

"By EDWARD P. BATES,

"CAROLINE S. BATES.

"To the Rev. Mary Baker Eddy,

"Boston, January 6, 1895."

Attached by a white ribbon to the scroll is a gold key to the church door.

The testimonial is encased in a white satin-lined box of rich green velvet.

The scroll is on exhibition in the window of J. C. Derby's jewelry store.

[*The Union Signal*, Chicago]

[Extract]

THE NEW WOMAN AND THE NEW CHURCH

The dedication, in Boston, of a Christian Science temple costing over two hundred thousand dollars, and for which the money was all paid in so that no debt had to be taken care of on dedication day, is a notable event. While we are not, and never have been, devotees of Christian Science, it becomes us as students of public questions not to ignore a movement which, starting fifteen years ago, has already gained to itself adherents in every part of the civilized world, for it is a significant fact that one cannot take up a daily paper in town or village—to say nothing of cities—without seeing notices of Christian Science meetings, and in most instances they are held at "headquarters."

We believe there are two reasons for this remarkable development, which has shown a vitality so unexpected. The first is that a revolt was inevitable from the crass materialism of the cruder science that had taken possession of men's minds, for as a wicked but witty writer has said, "If there were no God, we should be obliged to invent one." There is something in the constitution of man that requires the religious sentiment as much as his lungs call for breath; indeed, the breath of his soul is a belief in God.

But when Christian Science arose, the thought of the world's scientific leaders had become materialistically "lopsided," and this condition can never long continue.

1 There must be a righting-up of the mind as surely as of a
ship when under stress of storm it is ready to capsize. The
3 pendulum that has swung to one extreme will surely find
the other. The religious sentiment in women is so strong
that the revolt was headed by them; this was inevitable
6 in the nature of the case. It began in the most intellectual
city of the freest country in the world — that is to say,
it sought the line of least resistance. Boston is emphati-
9 cally the women's paradise, — numerically, socially, indeed every way. Here they have the largest individuality,
the most recognition, the widest outlook. Mrs. Eddy we
12 have never seen; her book has many a time been sent
us by interested friends, and out of respect to them we
have fairly broken our mental teeth over its granitic peb-
15 bles. That we could not understand it might be rather
to the credit of the book than otherwise. On this subject
we have no opinion to pronounce, but simply state the
18 fact.

We do not, therefore, speak of the system it sets forth,
either to praise or blame, but this much is true: the spirit
21 of Christian Science ideas has caused an army of well-mean-
ing people to believe in God and the power of faith, who
did not believe in them before. It has made a myriad of
24 women more thoughtful and devout; it has brought a
hopeful spirit into the homes of unnumbered invalids.
The belief that "thoughts are things," that the invisible
27 is the only real world, that we are here to be trained into
harmony with the laws of God, and that what we are here
determines where we shall be hereafter — all these ideas
30 are Christian.

The chimes on the Christian Science temple in Boston
played "All hail the power of Jesus' name," on the morning of the dedication. We did not attend, but we learn
that the name of Christ is nowhere spoken with more
reverence than it was during those services, and that he
is set forth as the power of God for righteousness and the
express image of God for love.

[*The New Century*, Boston, February, 1895]

ONE POINT OF VIEW — THE NEW WOMAN

We all know her — she is simply the woman of the past
with an added grace — a newer charm. Some of her
dearest ones call her "selfish" because she thinks so much
of herself she spends her whole time helping others. She
represents the composite beauty, sweetness, and nobility
of all those who scorn self for the sake of love and her
handmaiden duty — of all those who seek the brightness
of truth not as the moth to be destroyed thereby, but as
the lark who soars and sings to the great sun. She is of
those who have so much to give they want no time to take,
and their name is legion. She is as full of beautiful possibilities as a perfect harp, and she realizes that all the har-
monies of the universe are in herself, while her own soul
plays upon magic strings the unwritten anthems of love.
She is the apostle of the true, the beautiful, the good, com-
missioned to complete all that the twelve have left undone.
Hers is the mission of missions — the highest of all — to

1 make the body not the prison, but the palace of the soul,
with the brain for its great white throne.

3 When she comes like the south wind into the cold haunts
of sin and sorrow, her words are smiles and her smiles are
the sunlight which heals the stricken soul. Her hand is
6 tender — but steel tempered with holy resolve, and as
one whom her love had glorified once said — she is soft
and gentle, but you could no more turn her from her
9 course than winter could stop the coming of spring. She
has long learned with patience, and to-day she knows
many things dear to the soul far better than her teachers.
12 In olden times the Jews claimed to be the conservators
of the world's morals — they treated woman as a chattel,
and said that because she was created after man, she was
15 created solely for man. Too many still are Jews who
never called Abraham "Father," while the Jews themselves have long acknowledged woman as man's proper
18 helpmeet. In those days women had few lawful claims
and no one to urge them. True, there were Miriam and
Esther, but they sang and sacrificed for their people, not
21 for their sex.

To-day there are ten thousand Esthers, and Miriams
by the million, who sing best by singing most for their
24 own sex. They are demanding the right to help make
the laws, or at least to help enforce the laws upon
which depends the welfare of their husbands, their chil-
27 dren, and themselves. Why should our selfish self longer
remain deaf to their cry? The date is no longer B. C.
Might no longer makes right, and in this fair land at least
30 fear has ceased to kiss the iron heel of wrong. Why then

should we continue to demand woman's love and woman's help while we recklessly promise as lover and candidate what we never fulfil as husband and office-holder? In our secret heart our better self is shamed and dishonored, and appeals from Philip drunk to Philip sober, but has not yet the moral strength and courage to prosecute the appeal. But the east is rosy, and the sunlight cannot long be delayed. Woman must not and will not be disheartened by a thousand denials or a million of broken pledges. With the assurance of faith she prays, with the certainty of inspiration she works, and with the patience of genius she waits. At last she is becoming "as fair as the morn, as bright as the sun, and as terrible as an army with banners" to those who march under the black flag of oppression and wield the ruthless sword of injustice.

In olden times it was the Amazons who conquered the invincibles, and we must look now to their daughters to overcome our own allied armies of evil and to save us from ourselves. She must and will succeed, for as David sang — "God shall help her, and that right early." When we try to praise her later works it is as if we would pour incense upon the rose. It is the proudest boast of many of us that we are "bound to her by bonds dearer than freedom," and that we live in the reflected royalty which shines from her brow. We rejoice with her that at last we begin to know what John on Patmos meant — "And there appeared a great wonder in heaven, a woman clothed with the sun, and the moon under her feet, and upon her head a crown of twelve stars." She brought to warring men the Prince of Peace, and he, departing, left his scepter

1 not in her hand, but in her soul. "The time of times"
is near when "the new woman" shall subdue the whole
3 earth with the weapons of peace. Then shall wrong be
robbed of her bitterness and ingratitude of her sting,
revenge shall clasp hands with pity, and love shall dwell
6 in the tents of hate; while side by side, equal partners in
all that is worth living for, shall stand the new man with
the new woman.

————

9 [*Christian Science Journal*, January, 1895]
[Extract]

THE MOTHER CHURCH

12 The Mother Church edifice — The First Church of
Christ, Scientist, in Boston, is erected. The close of the
year, Anno Domini 1894, witnessed the completion of
15 "our prayer in stone," all predictions and prognostications
to the contrary notwithstanding.

Of the significance of this achievement we shall not
18 undertake to speak in this article. It can be better felt
than expressed. All who are awake thereto have some
measure of understanding of what it means. But only
21 the future will tell the story of its mighty meaning or un-
fold it to the comprehension of mankind. It is enough for
us now to know that all obstacles to its completion have
24 been met and overcome, and that our temple is completed
as God intended it should be.

This achievement is the result of long years of untiring,
27 unselfish, and zealous effort on the part of our beloved
teacher and Leader, the Reverend Mary Baker Eddy,
the Discoverer and Founder of Christian Science, who

nearly thirty years ago began to lay the foundation of
this temple, and whose devotion and consecration to God
and humanity during the intervening years have made
its erection possible.

Those who now, in part, understand her mission, turn
their hearts in gratitude to her for her great work, and
those who do not understand it will, in the fulness of time,
see and acknowledge it.   In the measure in which she has
unfolded and demonstrated divine Love, and built up in
human consciousness a better and higher conception of
God as Life, Truth, and Love, — as the divine Principle
of all things which really exist, — and in the degree in
which she has demonstrated the system of healing of Jesus
and the apostles, surely she, as the one chosen of God to
this end, is entitled to the gratitude and love of all who
desire a better and grander humanity, and who believe
it to be possible to establish the kingdom of heaven upon
earth in accordance with the prayer and teachings of
Jesus Christ.

[*Concord Evening Monitor*, March 23, 1895]

TESTIMONIAL AND GIFT

TO REV. MARY BAKER EDDY, FROM THE FIRST CHURCH OF CHRIST, SCIENTIST, IN BOSTON

Rev. Mary Baker Eddy received Friday, from the Christian Science Board of Directors, Boston, a beautiful and
unique testimonial of the appreciation of her labors and
loving generosity in the Cause of their common faith.   It
was a facsimile of the corner-stone of the new church of

1 the Christian Scientists, just completed, being of granite, about six inches in each dimension, and contains a solid

3 gold box, upon the cover of which is this inscription: —

"To our Beloved Teacher, the Reverend Mary Baker Eddy, Discoverer and Founder of Christian Science, from

6 her affectionate Students, the Christian Science Board of Directors."

On the under side of the cover are the facsimile sig-

9 natures of the Directors, — Ira O. Knapp, William B. Johnson, Joseph Armstrong, and Stephen A. Chase, with the date, "1895." The beautiful souvenir is en-

12 cased in an elegant plush box.

Accompanying the stone testimonial was the following address from the Board of Directors: —

15   Boston, March 20, 1895.

To the Reverend Mary Baker Eddy, our Beloved Teacher and Leader: — We are happy to announce to you

18 the completion of The First Church of Christ, Scientist, in Boston.

In behalf of your loving students and all contributors

21 wherever they may be, we hereby present this church to you as a testimonial of love and gratitude for your labors and loving sacrifice, as the Discoverer and Founder of

24 Christian Science, and the author of its textbook, "Science and Health with Key to the Scriptures."

We therefore respectfully extend to you the invitation

27 to become the permanent pastor of this church, in connection with the Bible and the book alluded to above, which you have already ordained as our pastor. And we

most cordially invite you to be present and take charge   1
of any services that may be held therein. We especially
desire you to be present on the twenty-fourth day of March,   3
eighteen hundred and ninety-five, to accept this offering,
with our humble benediction.

Lovingly yours,   6

Ira O. Knapp,   Joseph Armstrong,
William B. Johnson,   Stephen A. Chase,
    The Christian Science Board of Directors.   9

REV. MRS. EDDY'S REPLY

Beloved Directors and Brethren: — For your costly offering, and kind call to the pastorate of "The First Church   12
of Christ, Scientist," in Boston — accept my profound
thanks. But permit me, respectfully, to decline their ac-
ceptance, while I fully appreciate your kind intentions.   15
If it will comfort you in the least, make me your *Pastor
Emeritus*, nominally. Through my book, your textbook,
I already speak to you each Sunday. You ask too much   18
when asking me to accept your grand church edifice. I
have more of earth now, than I desire, and less of heaven;
so pardon my refusal of that as a material offering. More   21
effectual than the forum are our states of mind, to bless
mankind. This wish stops not with my pen — God give
you grace. As our church's tall tower detains the sun,   24
so may luminous lines from your lives linger, a legacy to
our race.

Mary Baker Eddy.   27

March 25, 1895.

1 LIST OF LEADING NEWSPAPERS WHOSE ARTICLES
ARE OMITTED

3 From Canada to New Orleans, and from the Atlantic
to the Pacific ocean, the author has received leading newspapers with uniformly kind and interesting articles on
6 the dedication of The Mother Church. They were, however, too voluminous for these pages. To those which are
copied she can append only a few of the names of other
9 prominent newspapers whose articles are reluctantly
omitted.

EASTERN STATES

12 *Advertiser*, Calais, Me.
Advertiser, Boston, Mass.
Farmer, Bridgeport, Conn.
15 *Independent*, Rockland, Mass.
Kennebec Journal, Augusta, Me.
News, New Haven, Conn.
18 *News*, Newport, R. I.
Post, Boston, Mass.
Post, Hartford, Conn.
21 *Republican*, Springfield, Mass.
Sentinel, Eastport, Me.
Sun, Attleboro, Mass.

24 MIDDLE STATES

Advertiser, New York City.
Bulletin, Auburn, N. Y.
27 *Daily*, York, Pa.
Evening Reporter, Lebanon, Pa.
Farmer, Bridgeport, Conn.
30 *Herald*, Rochester, N. Y.
Independent, Harrisburg, Pa.
Inquirer, Philadelphia, Pa.

1   *News-Tribune*, Duluth, Minn.
   Pioneer-Press, St. Paul, Minn.
3   *Post-Intelligencer*, Seattle, Wash.
   Salt Lake Herald, Salt Lake City, Utah.
   Sentinel, Indianapolis, Ind.
6   *Sentinel*, Milwaukee, Wis.
   Star, Kansas City, Mo.
   Telegram, Portland, Ore.
9   *Times*, Chicago, Ill.
   Times, Minneapolis, Minn.
   Tribune, Minneapolis, Minn.
12   *Tribune*, Salt Lake City, Utah.

   Free Press, London, Can.

CHRISTIAN SCIENCE
VERSUS
PANTHEISM